EDUCATION
AND
MODERN SPIRITUAL LIFE

EDUCATION AND MODERN SPIRITUAL LIFE

by

Rudolf Steiner

STEINERBOOKS
(A division of Garber Communications, Inc.)
Blauvelt, New York 10913, U.S.A.

Copyright © 1989 by Garber Communications, Inc.

All rights in this book are reserved. No part of this book may be reproduced in any form without written permission from the publishers except for brief quotations embodied in critical articles for reviews. For information, address Garber Communications, Inc., 5 Garber Hill Road, Blauvelt, NY 10913.

First American Revised Edition

Library of Congress Catalogue Card Number: 89-92083
International Standard Book Numbers:
0-89345-262-9 (paperbound)

This publication of this book has been made possible, in part, through the assistance of the *Steiner Institute for Spiritual Research,* Blauvelt, New York 10913.

Printed in the United States of America

PREFACE

This volume was originally printed in 1928, revised in 1943, and with further revisions by J. Darrell and an added lecture translated by George Adams, published in the present version in 1954 by the Anthroposophical Publishing Company of London, England.

This inspiring book, consisting of a total of fourteen lectures, a foreword, a summary of the contents of the lectures, is a unique experience that not only concerns itself with the education of children, but moves far beyond, into the human beings present-day Spiritual Life and its requirements.

The lectures, given as Ilkley, Yorkshire, England on August 5 through 17, 1923, were a continuation and expansion of a series of nine lectures given by Dr. Steiner the year before, in August, 1922, at Manchester College, Oxford, England. (*Spiritual Ground of Education,* Spiritual Science Library, Blauvelt, NY).

The following short excerpt from Dr. Guenther Wachsmuth's book, *The Life and Work of Rudolf Steiner* (pg. 507, Spiritual Science Library, Blauvelt, NY), points out the special emphasis and circumstances surrounding the course of lectures. One of these activities consisted of a course of thirteen lectures given on August 19 through 31, 1923 at Penmaenmawr, North Wales: *The Evolution of the World and of Humanity* (Spiritual Science Library, Blauvelt, NY).

"After Rudolf Steiner had provided and clarified his new directives in a number of countries in the north of Europe, he went at the beginning of August to England to strengthen and supplement what had been developed there and to prepare for the new duties. At first he devoted himself to carrying further the pedagogical work of the preceding year, giving a lecture on *Contemporary Spiritual Life and*

Education, at Ilkley, under the auspices of the "Union for the Realization of Spiritual Values in Education." Many distinguished personalities, not only of England but also from other European countries, took part in this course of lectures. Lively discussions between the lectures gave a manifestation of much stimulation. Dr. Steiner spoke also at a seminar for teachers before a large audience on methods in education. The presiding officer at this meeting was the Archdeacon of Halifax, who showed a marked objectivity and interest in new spiritual values. The lofty ethical value marking the pedagogical ideas of Dr. Steiner could evidently be realized by all who had open minds, and here in England this was strongly manifest."

Bernard J. Garber
September, 1989

CONTENTS

                                                          PAGE

I

Science, Art, Religion and Morality   24
    5th August, 1923

II

Principles of Greek Education   38
    6th August, 1923

III

Greek Education and the Middle Ages   54
    7th August, 1923

IV

The Connection of the Spirit with Bodily Organs   ..   70
    8th August, 1923

V

The Emancipation of the Will in the Human Organism   88
    9th August, 1923

VI

Walking, Speaking, Thinking   105
    10th August, 1923

VII

The Rhythmic System, Sleeping and Waking, Imitation   120
    11*th August*, 1923

VIII

Reading, Writing and Nature Study   135
    13*th August*, 1923

IX

Arithmetic, Geometry, History   152
    14*th August*, 1923

X

Physics, Chemistry, Handwork, Language, Religion   ..   168
    15*th August*, 1923

XI

Memory, Temperaments, Bodily Culture and Art   ..   182
    16*th August*, 1923

XII

Education Towards Inner Freedom   196
    17*th August*, 1923

SPECIAL LECTURE

Three Epochs in the Religious Education of Man   ..   213
    Sunday, 12*th August*, 1923

FAREWELL ADDRESS   226
    17*th August*, 1923 (*Evening*).

SUMMARY OF CONTENTS

I

SCIENCE, ART, RELIGION, MORALITY

Introductory

Education strives to work creatively upon the human being—nature's most sublime work of art. The onesidedness implied in the old term " Pedagogy " must be superseded. In modern times intellectual knowledge, art, religion and morality have grown apart from each other, but there was an age in which they were one. Modern science eliminates the element of art. Man's inner activity of thought has gradually been lost; he is content to let thoughts be aroused by external objects. The inner forces of thought form man from childhood on. Active thinking can rise to *Imagination* and become meditative knowledge, leading to art. When this kind of thinking has matured, it must be transcended by a moral act. The spiritual world may then enter man's consciousness as *Inspiration*, which can flow directly into art. Through art, man is then able to give expression to Divine Will; artistic creation becomes a divine office. Formerly, art could lead men directly to religion. All religion has proceeded from Inspiration. When man was aware of a divine-creative power within him, he was able to realise the presence of the God not only in the sanctuary but in the world. This is true morality. When man has found his place in the world of spirit through a life of true religion, *Intuition* imbues him with morality. We need this Intuition for the renewing of our civilization, in order that we may rediscover the harmony between science, art, religion and morality.

II

PRINCIPLES OF GREEK EDUCATION

The art of education must reckon with the historical course of human civilization, with the changes it has brought about in the souls of men. If man, as a being of body, soul and spirit, is to find his right place in social life, education must be founded on a knowledge of man as he is in the present epoch. Three stages in the development of education: (1) The Greek ideal was the *Gymnast* —one who knew how to express in the beauty of his bodily actions, the divine beauty of the cosmos. The separation of spirit, soul and body began with Roman culture. Training of the soul qualities, with bodily training in the background. (2) The *Rhetorician* was the ideal of medieval education. Halfway through the Middle Ages came the impulse to intellectualism. The man of knowledge, no longer the man of practical skill in action, was now the ideal of education. (3) In modern civilization the ideal is the *Doctor*, or *Professor*. The ideal of our own times is the " *Human Universal.*"

The culture of ancient Greece was a continuation of oriental civilization—body, soul and spirit are one. On earth, between birth and death, soul and spirit live in the body. The work of the Gymnast carried further the deeply spiritual philosophy of the East. " Orchestric," song and the playing of the zither. Their connection with the systems of breathing and blood circulation in man. " Palestric " and intellectual development.

III

GREEK EDUCATION AND THE MIDDLE AGES

Significance of education at home up to the age of seven. The natural forces of growth and the being of soul and spirit are not as yet separate. They are a unity up to the seventh year. This inner force in the child is active in the pushing upward of the second teeth. After the change of teeth, certain forces are withdrawn from the body that the soul may develop the finer forces of her life. After puberty, the spirit is made manifest at the expense of the soul. The Greek saw the child of seven as a spiritual being who had descended into a physical body. After the seventh year, this being descends a second step, acquiring an earthly sheath of its own; before this age, pre-earthly forces have been working in the body. The task of the Gymnast was to understand the divine forces working in the human body and to develop them further.

The peoples streaming in from the East, who founded medieval civilization, brought the new consciousness of the unworthiness of slavery; greater respect was paid to woman; the idea of "Faith" superseded the primal wisdom that had previously poured through man. Primal wisdom became tradition that must be memorised.

The Gymnast sought to preserve the forces of childhood until the time of earthly death. Musical talent developed naturally from breathing and blood circulation; intellectual thinking from gymnastics; a marvellous memory from habitual bodily activities. The experience of individual consciousness (which emerges only after the age of puberty) began in the Middle Ages. The experience of inner freedom.

IV

THE CONNECTION OF THE SPIRIT WITH BODILY ORGANS

We must now reach a concrete understanding of the spirit. To-day we theorize about the spirit. We have a skeleton of spirit as the result of intellectual thinking. Thoughts must be brought to life, then they become whole. Ideals must cease to be abstract, they must feel and will in us. An example of the working of spirit in the body. The teeth develop not merely for the purposes of eating and speaking, but also in order that the faculty of thinking may emerge. After the change of teeth, the corresponding physical force appears as the power of thought. The physical force hitherto concentrated in the organs now becomes a force of soul. Living thought alone can understand these truths. Through Imaginative knowledge we understand the relation of man's etheric body to the surrounding universe. Some of these etheric forces are freed when the child gets his second teeth, and they then become the forces of thought. Dental sounds and thought.

A transformation of the whole being takes place between the seventh and fourteenth years. Puberty is merely an outer symptom of this transformation. Feeling has been freed from the bodily nature. The larynx and breast express this in their changing form. At puberty, the astral nature becomes independent of the body. To perceive the astral nature, Inspiration must be added to Imagination. The teacher has to aid this second supersensible member of man's being to become independent.

It is the task of the teacher gradually to make speech free of the bodily nature. At the age of seven years, organic activity is expressed in the labial sounds; at the age of fourteen, the soul-quality of feeling pours into the formation of the labials. Transition from organic to soul activity. A truly religious attitude must arise if the spirit in feeling is brought to the child and only this can penetrate to the full reality of the spirit.

V

EMANCIPATION OF THE WILL IN THE HUMAN ORGANISM

Until about the twentieth year the will is highly dependent on organic activity. At about the twenty-first year, the will becomes free. Until this age the human being is strongly subject to the forces of earthly gravity and struggles with them. An upward impulse then strikes into his blood. The direction of the will is from below upwards; of thinking, from above downwards. If the life of feeling is rightly developed between the ages of seven and fourteen, these two streams of force harmonize, and with them, thinking and willing. In man, this process is of the nature of a moral act. In their gymnastics, the Greeks stimulated the flow of force from head to limbs. We must learn to understand the sense in which the will becomes free within the organs of movement at the twenty-first year of life. This will fill us with reverence for the process of man's development, and then we can educate in the true sense.

The first line of St. John's Gospel. To the Greeks, the "Word" was a direct call to the human will. The Word lived in the movements of the human body. The Word embraced all natural phenomena, was creative. The Word, the Logos sounded through the whole cosmos. Greek gymnastics were an expression of the Word. Musical education contained an echo of the Word. The Word was active in Greek wrestling; in the Greek dance there was an echo of the Word in the element of music. Spirit worked right down into the being of man. Then came the Middle Ages. The dead Word was offered to man in the Latin language. Human feeling died to the living essence of the Logos, as contained in the Gospel of St. John. This lack is felt to-day and is the cause of the many demands for educational reforms. We have lost the spirit in the Word. In olden times the spirit was imminent in the Word. But the Word became an "idol"—this was the beginning of intellectualism. Man turned away from the Logos to the world of sense. The new era in education will begin with the rediscovery of the spirit of the Word, in the sense of the Gospel of St. John.

VI

Walking, Speaking, Thinking

Living ideas pass over into will and deed. The education of the child must begin directly after birth. This means that education is a concern of the whole of humanity. The first three years of life are the most important for the whole of future development. At first the child is one great sense-organ. His sense of taste is spread over the whole of his being. Forces that in the adult are localised in the different senses, are spread over the child's whole organism. In the child, spirit, soul and body are not separate; everything in the environment is imitated. Three fundamental faculties acquired by the child during the first three years of life: walking, speaking, thinking. To walk means to adjust oneself to the directions of space. The forces of orientation issue from organic impulses. The adult may not exercise the slightest coercion; he must be a helper only. If we follow with inner love every manifestation of human nature in the child, we stimulate health-bringing forces within him. The faculty of speech develops from the process of orientation in space; it arises from man's organism of movement. Speaking is thus an outcome of walking. The forces of movement are carried over to the head structure; this is revealed in speech. As we help the child to speak we must be inwardly true, for the truthfulness of speech is absorbed by the physical organism. The delicate process of in-breathing and out-breathing is imitated by the child. The capacity to change oxygen into carbonic acid in the more intimate regions of human life in the right way depends upon whether we have been handled truthfully or untruthfully during the time we were learning to speak. Thinking arises in turn out of speech. Since the child is one great sense-organ and imitates the spiritual in his physical being, clarity and precision must permeate our own thinking if we are to help the child in this connection. Confused thinking in the child's environment is the primary cause of nervous troubles. Diseases connected with the metabolic process are the result of being unwisely taught to walk. Digestive disturbances may be the outcome of untruthfulness in the way the child has been taught to speak; nervous troubles result from confused thinking.

Inner as well as outer punishment can be inflicted on the child. We must help to build up the child's brain like a sculptor who works on his medium with mobile, delicate hand. The child's play. Artistic qualities of playthings. If we give intellectual training to the child before the fourth or fifth years we shall bring him up to be a materialist. He must be left in his gentle, dream-like existence as long as possible.

VII

THE RHYTHMIC SYSTEM. SLEEPING AND WAKING. IMITATION

Man is an imitative being up to the time of the change of teeth, and the effects of this imitation continue in his physical constitution through the whole of earthly life. Up to the age of seven the child is an inner sculptor: the formative forces proceed from the head and give shape to the whole being. The moral qualities observed in the environment play a part in building up the system of veins, blood circulation, breathing, and so forth, although much may be corrected in later life by moral strength. The rhythmic system is of paramount importance after the change of teeth. The whole teaching at this age must bear a rhythmic quality. We help the child to breathe in a healthy way if we bring an artistic quality into the teaching. An educational attitude, drawing on a thorough knowledge of man, becomes an art of education. There is little artistic feeling in modern civilization. An artistic conception of civilization as a whole can lead to principles of health-bringing education. In the first period of life (to the age of seven) the child is an inner sculptor; after the seventh year these plastic forces become forces of soul. The child must be taught pictorially, and there must be a musical interplay between teacher and child. Intellectual training must follow artistic development. The child must be taught to use his intellect, but it must never be forced. The rhythm of sleeping and waking. The rhythmic system never tires. Intellect and will cause fatigue. Teaching that is permeated by an artistic quality flows into the rhythmic system. To coerce the child to think is to generate forces connected with salt-deposits and the forming of bone. Thus, if writing is taught in a purely intellectual way, the tendency to sclerosis in later life is set up. From the artistic qualities that are brought into play in drawing and painting, we can lead over from the picture to the concept or idea. Working from the basis of the artistic, we can educate the human being in such a way that he will feel a sense of inner well-being with every step and every movement of the hand. Artistic teaching works on the waking life. Bodily activity works upon the life of sleep. The nature of will. In the activity of willing, a process of combustion is set up in the organism, and this can only be regulated in sleep. Purely conventional exercises for the body prevent the child from getting the deep, sound sleep that is necessary for the regeneration of the organism. Artistic activity prompts impulses to right bodily activity. Care of the body in education.

After the seventh year the principle of education must be that of natural authority. Only after the age of fourteen is the child ready to form personal judgments.

VIII

Reading, Writing and Nature Study

Characteristic examples of the way in which writing of consonants should be taught. Vowels are an expression of the inner being. Eurhythmy helps with the vowels. Reading and the development of conceptual life. Between the ninth and tenth years, the child begins to make a distinction between himself and the outer world. Before this all outer things must be so described that they seem to speak as living beings to the child. Plant teaching. The earth as a living being. Up to the twelfth year the child has no interest in or understanding of mineral substance. From plant teaching we lead on to geography. Through a right teaching about the plants we develop in the child a living, not a dead intellect. Animal teaching. The animal kingdom in its connection with man. Man is the synthesis of the animal species spread over the earth. Threefold structure of man and the animal forms. Man bears the spirit within him and thus is raised above the animal world. This living conception of the relation of man to the animal world strengthens the will. Thus in teaching about plants and animals education passes over into the development of thinking and willing. The healthy relationship between thinking, feeling and willing.

IX

ARITHMETIC, GEOMETRY, HISTORY

Painting, drawing, writing, plant teaching, arithmetic and geometry affect the child's etheric body as well as his physical body. The etheric body preserves the after-effects of these activities during sleep. Animal-teaching, history and the like, are taken up by the astral body and ego into the spiritual world during sleep. Arithmetic and geometry affect the whole man. Geometry and concrete conceptions of space. The right way to teach arithmetic. One particular subject should be continued for three or four weeks, and we should then pass on to another. This reckons with the unconscious in man. History should be taught in a living way. The child has no understanding of causality until he has reached the age of twelve. Our teaching of history must appeal to the child's life of feeling and will. Preparation of the subject-matter of the lessons.

X

Physics, Chemistry, Crafts, Language, Religion

Teaching in connection with minerals and stones should not begin until the child has reached the age of eleven or twelve. Physics and chemistry work upon the intellect alone. Only at this age should the child be taught the relation between cause and effect and the so-called "objective" connections in history and geography. At about fourteen chemistry and physics should pass over into spinning, weaving, technical chemistry. Knowledge of surrounding technical world must now begin. Thus the child is led rightly into social life.

Speech and its connection with the whole being of man. How to teach languages. Consciousness becomes self-consciousness between the ninth and tenth years. This is the age when we can begin to teach the rules of grammar and syntax.

In all religious instruction we must bear in mind the particular age of the child. At first he must be taught to understand the Divine-Spiritual imminent in the world. If we have so taught him about plants, clouds, springs, and the like that his whole environment seems to live, we can easily pass on to the divine "Father Principle." Gratitude and love. Not until the child has reached the age of ten ought we to begin to speak of duty. At this age we can lead him on to have some understanding of the Mystery of Golgotha.

XI

Memory, Temperaments, Bodily Culture and Art

The right way in which to develop the child's memory. Three golden rules. The teacher must have an intuitive understanding of certain symptoms of health and disease in the child. Treatment of children according to their particular temperaments. Contact between parents and teachers. Ungifted children should move upward with the class. Special class in the Waldorf School for backward children. Individual treatment necessary in this. The teacher must observe his children. Curative eurhythmy. The moment we begin to teach the child physics and chemistry, we must add some form of artistic work and, most essentially, help towards artistic understanding as a counterbalance. Plastic work develops all-round observation. Plastic work and the understanding of plants. Music and the understanding of animals. The artistic must come into education if civilisation is to advance. Art is not a mere invention of man; it is a domain in which the human being is able to gaze into the secrets of nature at a level different from that of ordinary thought.

XII

Education Towards Inner Freedom, Eurhythmy, Teachers' Meetings

Art and science, taught in the right way, lead to a deepening of moral and religious life. The union of knowing and doing. The bodily nature is a revelation of the spiritual and the spiritual is striving to work creatively in the body. The idea must pass into the child's feeling-life and so into the will. Handwork. Eurhythmy, a visible speech. Contrast between eurhythmy and gymnastics. The College of Teachers. Teachers' Meetings. Evening meetings for parents.

XIII

THREE EPOCHS IN THE RELIGIOUS EDUCATION OF MAN

XIV

FAREWELL ADDRESS

Anthroposophy and the Waldorf School. Anthroposophy has no desire to be dogmatic but strives to understand the world in its true reality. The transition from the Intellectual to the Spiritual Soul. The development of free spiritual activity. Transition in fourteenth century from Latin to national languages. To-day, medium of international understanding must be thought not language. This thought to be found in Anthroposophy. World economy has made the body: Anthroposophy seeks to be soul and spirit of this body.

FOREWORD

RUDOLF STEINER'S ART OF EDUCATION

The science of Anthroposophy, embracing a knowledge of man as microcosm within the macrocosm and of his whole cosmic being, has been given us by Rudolf Steiner in a form suitable for the modern age—and he alone was able to inaugurate a new art of education founded on a profound knowledge of man and his divine origin. How can education become an art if there is no vision of the mysteries behind the outward revelations of man, if there is knowledge only of the exterior form and not of his essential being, of the sheath and not the kernel, of semblance and not truth—if, above all, people fear to take the first step towards this truth ? Rudolf Steiner schools do not teach a particular conception of things—that has nothing to do with the children—and do not want to do so. Their aim is to enable the child to develop and unfold in freedom out of his own nature. The child should live in an element of soul and spirit that is at once a support and help, instead of being allowed to sink into a spiritual void, finally emerging from school life wearied in soul and body. Those who teach, however, must certainly possess a conception of the world that enables them in renewed freshness to grapple with the problems of education and fills them with reverence and devotion, so that they may help the child to overcome any hereditary failings and unfold the divine seed within him. A body of teachers borne onwards by these impulses can collectively overcome their individual weaknesses and correct the faults that are inevitably a part of all human strivings. The knowledge imparted by Rudolf Steiner to the teachers around him has such world-transforming power that it will be able to change man himself—potentially the most resistant element in all creation. It works upon the yet immature element of soul like rain in spring, rousing the earth from its confines by its impelling warmth. This wisdom contained in the art of education inaugurated by Rudolf Steiner is as immune from death as the soft radiance of the Christmas Folk-Plays he restored to us at Dornach and taught us to love. Those who try to put this wisdom into practice may indeed fall into all kinds of errors, into sentimentality and the like, but its heart of truth is so strong that should this alone remain, all such incidental failings will ultimately be overcome.

This new art of education is concerned with the possibilities latent in the whole being of man and reckons, at the same time, with the conditions of modern life. At the central point stands man—no longer a masculine being, or a creed, or a class, but man. Our present age needs and is waiting for an education concerned with the universal-human element in man, arising from the necessities of the times, free from all distinctions of class, sex and creed, conscious only of the demands which modern life imposes on us. Our social life needs a new impulse, but one arising out of the past as a blossom from a plant. Collapse of itself brings no new life. Isolated reforms no longer avail in a cultural life that is self-destructive in its nature. A new orientation is necessary. Only a new orientation directed out of the inner forces of the human being as they appear through the epochs of civilization will avail—and a new knowledge of man's being.

This world-embracing knowledge is here to-day, in a form so intelligible to modern modes of thought that it lies within the power of all who are able and willing to think clearly. They have but to put aside bias and prejudice and explore the paths already made for them. Life to-day demands wide, all-round vision, not the narrow perspectives of specialized branches of science; it demands to be freed from itself from the unenlightened inertia that has fallen upon spheres of cultures once quickened by the spirit. The pressing task of to-day is to bring the spirit into these spheres once again. The tree of ancient human culture is threatened by the axe from the East, and will fall if it has not the powerful forces with which to withstand it. The cold, ruthless intelligence that is the instrument of this menacing destiny has a truly demoniacal cleverness and breadth of vision, and its gaze is directed to the future which the coming generation will bring to birth. The fact that with their hypnotic methods of education and their compulsive slogans they are destroying that noblest of all good things and the hardest to win, the freedom of the human ego, troubles them not at all; their one concern is to secure instruments for the attainment of their own ends. " Reasonable compulsion " is a phrase that is now placed side by side with " the end justifies the means." The methods adopted by Soviet Russia for the radical extermination of spirit will produce a race of men already perilously near to animality, more brutal and destructive than ever before. The power of this destructive spirit is spreading over Asia and has already infected China; the ancient spirituality of the East is being undermined and threatened with ruin; age-old civilizations, maintained by spiritual forces, by the recognition among the masses of divine commands and the laws of destiny, will be overthrown by a cataclysm if this ancient spirituality is thus swept away by these passions, and then the storm will break over the West. And if this comes to pass, with what will the German peoples be able to oppose these forces of destruction?

Only with the forces of a spiritual life united with the divine power of the ego. A return to ancient piety, to faith and submissiveness will no longer help. Nor will processions, prayers and penances avail—such methods have long been practised, and with greater intensity in the East than in the West. One thing alone can face the dangers that are threatening: knowledge living in the ego made strong by freedom, grasping with conscious certainty of purpose all that faith has abandoned and the dreams of the mystic have been unable to save. Far removed from ecstacy or fanaticism —which have already played their part in the development of man's sentient life—from all danger of a reversion to the adoration of relics and the tendency to materialize spiritual values, above all from methods leading to repression of self-consciousness for the sake of tangible evidence of the spirit —the narrow way mounts up by which man may return to true spirituality. Following this path he can, by consciously acquiring new powers of spiritual knowledge and embodying them in his will, regain the knowledge lost to him during the development of his personality. When body and soul are once again pervaded with spirit, the human ego will have ascended to the Divine ego. Then Europe will be able to discharge her debt to Asia and then—perhaps—she may be spared the last penalties of the revenge for her material conquest of the East. This vengeance threatens to-day. Our children will have to face it and must be prepared.

Spirit is power, spirit is health. Children educated in the spirit that is mightier than the powers of negation, of revolution, of chaos, of atheism, may form a human bulwark against the forces of destruction. Why was the little Greek race able to stem the torrent of the Persian invasion? Because all its forces were unfolded from out of the deep spiritual knowledge possessed by its leaders and teachers; because its education reckoned with the demands of the times, beholding in the body an expression of spirit, knowing that the spirit worked with greatest strength when the creative forces of the body were unhindered and could continue to develop in freedom. What does Rudolf Steiner tell us in these lectures—given to an English audience in a country whose engrossment in sport must be described as one of its limitations ?—The body was the starting-point of all Greek education. Our point of departure must be the spirit. The paths leading from the spirit also to the education of the body must be found. Education to-day is almost entirely intellectualism, lacking any true insight into the being of man. The Greek took his start from physical man standing there before him; we in our age must start from a human ideal. Greek education preserved the growth-forces of early childhood in freshness and vigour on into old age. " Divine Gymnastic " was to be continued by education. To find the true impulse of our age we must observe the signs of the time. We have to educate free men and women. Slavery, the seclusion of woman, ancient traditional wisdom—these were no longer compatible with the consciousness of man even in the Middle Ages, where the life of soul was given the foremost place and education was based on tradition and faith. The firm foundations in which Greek gymnastic had been rooted began to waver and to be dependent on the individual tact of the teacher. To-day we grope in the dark —it is an age of experiment and theoretical reform. The new orientation must proceed from the spirit, from the knowledge of the reality of the spirit active in the cosmos and in man. This makes a new and definite demand upon us in the present age if we would stand rightly in a new social life. The art of education in ancient Greece was the outcome of its whole civilization and reflected the essential nature of Greek culture. To-day we do not help the child to find his feet in the world with an awakened understanding of social conditions. The growing human being has to find his place in social life and to this end he must be made familiar with the manifold creations of the human mind. The place which the human being will assume in the social order has, first, to be a matter of conscious realization. A spiritual understanding of man can alone enable this self-consciousness to mature at the proper time. The consciousness of individual freedom does not awaken until after the age of fourteen. It was less intense in the Greek, whose education was still a continuation of the nature-processes within the human being. Education in our day must be a moral achievement; we must develop intuition, we must be pioneers of a future humanity. We must strive to make education of the free man into a free act, i.e., a moral act of the highest order.

Again and again Rudolf Steiner urged the necessity of a fundamental knowledge of man's being, for no education can flourish on the soil of abstract theories; it must be rooted in realities and by way of these realities the spirit finds its way into human life. To-day we endeavour to grasp the spirit only by means of ideas. Man, however, does not merely think; he also feels and wills, and we must view him in his full manhood. In our thought we must approach the human being as a work of art; if we are to come with the spiritual in our feelings, a religious mood—amounting almost to that of ritual—must be added to this artistic perception. The teacher must be an artist through and through, permeated with a deep vein of piety. He must be truly moral as he helps to form the child's character, for this will mean to harmonise the faculties of thought and will. The fact that here on earth man can unite his will with his thought, makes him a moral being. The fundamental problem of all education is to bring man's thinking and willing into harmony.

The teaching as a whole must be full of an artistic quality, but over and above this a counterbalance to the materialistic conceptions of natural science must be created by the development of a living understanding of art. If the human being learns to view the world as a great work of art, to see nature as a creative artist, he is ready for the development of the religious sense. Teaching must be a kind of balance, holding in one scale all those elements that bind man to the earth—and in the other, everything that leads to art, sublimating into spirit all that has been worked out and elaborated in ordinary life.

A religious deepening of the whole being is one of the essential tasks of education. Moral and religious qualities inhere in the child's life of feeling when he realizes that the bodily nature is everywhere a manifestation of the spiritual, and that the spiritual is ever seeking to enter creatively into the body. Living sympathies and antipathies for good and evil, delight in goodness, abhorrence of evil—these qualities, not precepts or injunctions, make the child a truly moral being. With the development of his sense of freedom and individual power of discrimination at the age of fifteen or sixteen, such feelings will then arise of themselves. He will be immune from outside influence and be able to form his own free judgments. Conventional rules and regulations are of no avail. We must work, at the right age, on the child's life of feeling and perception—but not by way of dogma and mental concepts. Then no fetters will limit the individual power of judgment that emerges later. If the child has been educated in a wholly human sense, he will learn to feel and know his full manhood. His own free religious and moral nature will have been awakened. Our highest endeavour must be to develop free human beings who are able of themselves to impart purpose and direction to their lives.

I have tried to give a brief summary of the lectures given by Rudolf Steiner in Ilkley, printed here from shorthand reports. Such is the train of thought around which moves a life so rich that it probably could not, in the first place, have been offered to Germans—whose outstanding characteristic is a scrupulous pursuit of abstract concepts. In England and on the Continent, Rudolf Steiner spoke differently; he counted on the feeling for reality living in the English and relied on their power to receive an abundance of spiritual treasure. In the treatment of his subjects he constantly selected different points of departure, and in these lectures on education, he began with the culture of the body in Greece, because this is appropriate in a land where so much value is set upon the training of the body, even if this is done without insight into spiritual connections, and so is not truly progressive. There was yet another reason why, in England, Rudolf Steiner could enter so deeply into spiritual realities and carry his eager listeners with him. He was speaking in places still fragrant with the breath of ancient spirituality—a breath quickening speaker and audience alike. Side by side with religious conventionality and engrossment in business and comfort, the conservation of ancient spirituality has been possible in that land where material culture has made such strides. These two streams do not intermingle; they flow side by side. In other regions of the earth, too, spirit and body have lost the way to one another. Education cannot thrive under these conditions and men will inevitably find themselves more and more unstable or more and more hardened, if Rudolf Steiner's educational impulse is not recognized and followed. . . . " Our present age needs an art of education whereby the form-building spirit, the sentient spirit, the will-sustaining spirit, may again be brought to man."

MARIE STEINER.

I

SCIENCE, ART, RELIGION AND MORALITY

My first words must be a reply to the kind greeting given by Miss Beverley to Frau Doctor Steiner and myself, and I can assure you that we deeply appreciate the invitation to give this course of lectures. My essential task will be to show what Anthroposophy has to say on the subject of education and to describe the attempt already made in the Waldorf School at Stuttgart to apply the educational principles arising out of Anthroposophy. We gladly accepted the invitation to come to the North of England and it gives me deep satisfaction to speak on a subject which I consider so important, the more so as I am also speaking to those who have arranged this course and are not listening to lectures on this subject from this point of view for the first time. I hope, therefore, that more lies behind this conference than just the resolve of those who organized it, but that it may be taken as evidence that our previous activities are bearing fruit in current world-strivings.

English friends of Anthroposophy were with us at a conference held at Christmas, last year but one, when the Goetheanum—since taken from us by fire—was still standing. The conference was arranged by Mrs. Mackenzie, the author of an able book on the educational principles laid down by Hegel, and the sympathetic appreciation expressed there makes one hope that it is not, after all, so very difficult to find understanding that transcends the limits of nationality. What I myself said about education at the conference did not, of course, emanate from the more intellectualistic philosophy of Hegel, but from Anthroposophy, the nature of which is wholly spiritual. But again it was Mrs. Mackenzie who found that out of Anthroposophy, which while taking full account of Hegel passes beyond his intellectuality into the spiritual, something fruitful for education could be won.

Then I was able to speak of our educational principles and their practical application a second time last year, in the old university town of Oxford. And perhaps I am justified in thinking that those lectures, which amongst other things, dealt with how education is related to the social life, may have induced quite a number of English people concerned with education to visit our Waldorf School at Stuttgart. It was a great joy to welcome them there within the classrooms of our Waldorf school, amid the work of educating and teaching going on in those rooms, and we were delighted to hear that they were satisfied with our work and were following it with interest. During the visit the idea of holding this Summer Course on education seems to have arisen. Its roots, therefore, may be said to lie in previous activities and this very fact gives one the right confidence and the right courage as we embark upon the present lectures. Courage and confidence are necessary when one has to speak of matters still so unfamiliar to the spiritual life of to-day and in face of such strong opposition as comes from many quarters. More especially are they necessary when one attempts to explain principles that would approach, in a creative sense, the greatest artistic achievement of the cosmos —man himself.

Those who visited us will have realized how essentially Waldorf School education gets to grips with the deepest fibres of modern life. The educational methods applied there can really no longer be described by the word " pedagogy "—a treasured word which the Greeks learnt from Plato and the Platonists who had devoted themselves so sincerely to all educational questions. Pedagogy is, indeed, no longer an apt term to-day, for it shows straightaway the onesidedness of its ideals, and those who visited the Waldorf School will have realized this from the first. It is not, of course, unusual to-day, to find boys and girls educated together in the same classes and taught in the same way, and

I merely mention this to show you that in this respect, too, the methods of the Waldorf School are in line with recent developments.

What does the word " pedagogy " suggest ? The " pedagogue " is a teacher of boys. This shows us at once that in ancient Greece education was very one-sided. One half of humanity was excluded from serious education. To the Greek, the boy alone was man and the girl must stay in the background when it was a question of serious education. The pedagogue was a teacher of boys, concerned only with that sex.

In our times, the presence of girl-pupils in the schools is no longer unusual, although indeed it involves a radical change from customs by no means very ancient. Another feature of the Waldorf School, however, will even to-day have something strange about it for many people: not only are boys and girls there equal as pupils, but also on the teaching staff no distinction of sex is made, no distinction at any rate in principle, even up to the highest classes. Universally human considerations laid it upon us to get rid of this onesidedness. We had first to give up all that was in the old term " pedagogy," if we wanted to establish an education in accordance with modern conditions. That is only one aspect of an educational onesidedness implied by the name. Speaking in the broadest sense, it must be said that until recently nothing at all was known in education of man as such. Indeed, many onesided views have been held in the educational world—not only that of the separation of the sexes.

When the years of schooling according to the old principles were over, did man as such then step forth from them ? Never! To-day, however, mankind is preparing to seek for man, for pure, undimmed, undifferentiated humanity. That this had to be striven for can be seen from the way in which the Waldorf School was formed.

The first idea was to provide an education for children whose parents were working in the Waldorf-Astoria Factory, and as the Director was a member of the Anthroposophical Society, he asked me to arrange this education. I myself could do this only on the basis of Anthroposophy. And so, in the first place, the Waldorf School arose as a school for humanity as such, fashioned, it could in fact be said, out of the working-class. It was only "anthroposophical" in the sense that the man who first had the idea of the school happened to be an Anthroposophist. Here then, we have an educational institution arising on a social basis, that seeks to found the whole spirit and method of its teaching upon Anthroposophy. It was not in the remotest a question, however, of founding an "anthroposophical" school. On the contrary, we hold that because Anthroposophy can at all times efface itself, it is able to institute a school on universal-human principles and not upon the basis of social rank, philosophical conceptions or any other speciality.

This may well have occurred to those who visited the Waldorf School; and it can occur to one in every single thing that is done there. It may also have led to the invitation to give these present lectures. And in this introductory lecture, when I am not yet speaking of education, let me cordially thank all those who have arranged this Summer Course. I would also thank them for having arranged performances of eurhythmy which has already become such an integral part of Anthroposophy. At the very beginning let me express this hope: A Summer Course has brought us together. We have gathered together in a beautiful spot in the North of England, far away from the busy life of the winter months. You have given up your time of summer recreation to hear of subjects that will play an important part in the life of the future, and the time must come when the spirit uniting us now for a fortnight during the summer holidays will inspire all our winter work. I cannot adequately express my gratitude for the fact that you have dedicated your holidays to the study of ideas significant for the future. Just as sincerely as I thank you for this now, so do I trust that the spirit of our Summer Course may be carried on into the winter months—for only so can this Course bear real fruit.

Allow me to refer to the impressive words of Miss Macmillan yesterday, in which a deep social and pedagogical impulse found expression, and which in a sense bore witness that profound moral impulses must be sought for, if human civilization as a whole is to make further progress in education. When we allow the significance of such an impulse to work deeply in our hearts, we are led to the most fundamental problems in modern spiritual life—problems connected with the forms assumed by our culture and civilization in the course of human history. We are living in an age when certain spheres of culture, though standing in a measure side by side, are yet separated from one another. In the first place we have all that man can learn of the world through knowledge—communicated, for the most part, by the intellect alone. Then there is the sphere of art, where man tries to give expression to profound inner experiences, imitating with his human powers a divine creative activity. Again we have the religious strivings, the religious longings of man, wherein he seeks to unite the roots of his own existence with those of the universe. Lastly, we try to bring forth from within ourselves impulses which place us as moral beings in the civilized life of the world. In effect we confront four branches of culture: knowledge, art, religion, morality. But the course of human evolution has brought it about that these four branches are developing separately, and we no longer realize their common roots. It is of no value to criticize these conditions; they are necessities, but they must be understood.

To-day, therefore, we will remind ourselves of the beginnings of civilization. There was an ancient period in human evolution when science, art, religion, and the moral life were one. It was an age when the intellect had not yet developed its present abstract nature and when man sought to solve the riddles of existence by a kind of picture-consciousness. Mighty pictures stood there before his soul—pictures which in decadent form have since come down to us as myth and saga. Originally they proceeded from actual experience and knowledge of the spiritual content of the universe. There was indeed an age when in this direct, inner life of pictorial, imaginative vision man could perceive the spiritual foundations of the world of sense. And what his instinctive imagination thus gleaned from the universe, he made substantial by using earthly matter and so evolving architecture, sculpture, painting, music, and other arts. He embodied the fruits of his knowledge to his heart's delight in outer material forms. With his human faculties man copied divine creation, giving visible form to all that had first flowed into him as science and knowledge. In short, his art mirrored before the senses all that his forces of knowledge had first assimilated. In weakened form we find this faculty once again in Goethe, when out of his own knowledge and artistic conviction he spoke these significant words: " Beauty is a manifestation of the secret laws of nature, without which they would remain for ever hidden from us." And again: " He before whom nature begins to unveil her open secrets is conscious of an irresistible yearning for art, nature's worthiest expression."

Such a conception shows that man is fundamentally predisposed to view both science and art as two aspects of one and the same truth. This he could do in primeval ages, when knowledge brought him inner satisfaction as it arose in the forms of ideas before his soul, and when the beauty that enchanted him could be made visible to his senses in the arts—for experiences such as these were the essence of earlier civilizations.

What is our position to-day? As a result of all that intellectual abstractions have brought in their train we build up scientific systems of knowledge from which, as far as possible, art is eliminated. It is felt to be positively sinful to introduce art in any way into science, and anyone who is found guilty of this in a scientific book is at once condemned as a dilettante. Our knowledge must be sober, it must be objective, so it is said. Art may only supply what has nothing to do with objectivity, but only arises from the arbitrary will of man. A deep abyss thus opens between knowledge and art, and man no longer finds any means of crossing it. But it is to his own undoing that he no longer finds a means of crossing it. When he applies the science that is valued because of its freedom from art, he is led indeed to a marvellous knowledge of nature—but of nature devoid of life. The wonderful achievements of science are fully acknowledged by us, yet science is dumb before the mystery of man. Look where you will in science to-day, you will find wonderful answers to the problems of outer nature, but no answers to the riddle of man. The laws of science cannot come at him. Why is this? Heretical as it sounds to modern ears, this is the reason: The moment we draw near to the human being with the laws of nature, we must pass over into the realm of art. A heresy indeed, for people will certainly say: "That is no longer science. If you try to understand the human being by the artistic sense, you are not following the laws of observation and strict logic to which you must always adhere." However emphatically it may be held that this approach to man is unscientific because it is artistic, man is none the less an artistic creation of nature. All kinds of arguments may be advanced to the effect that this way of artistic understanding is thoroughly unscientific, but the fact remains that man cannot be grasped by purely scientific modes of cognition. And so—in spite of all our science—we come to a halt before the human being. Only if we are sufficiently unbiassed can we realise that we must turn to something else, that scientific intellectuality must here be allowed to pass over into the domain of art. Science itself must become art if we would approach the secrets of man's being.

Now if we follow this path with all our inner forces of soul, not only observing in an outwardly artistic sense, but taking the appropriate path of development, we can allow scientific intellectuality to flow over into what I have described as *Imagination* in my book, *Knowledge of the Higher Worlds and its Attainment*. This " Imaginative Knowledge " —to-day an object of such suspicion and opposition—is indeed possible when the kind of thinking that otherwise gives itself up passively to the outer world, a thinking more and more prevalent to-day, is roused to a living and positive activity. The difficulty of speaking of these things to-day is not that one is speaking about or against the scientific habits of our age, but that at bottom, when one goes into it, one is speaking against the whole of modern civilization. There is an increasing tendency to-day to disregard activity in thinking, inward, active participation in it, and surrendering oneself to the sequence of events to let thinking just run on in their train, without doing anything in the matter oneself.

This state of affairs began with the demand for material demonstration in spiritual things. Take the case of a lecture on spiritual subjects. Visible evidence is out of the question, because words are the only available media—one cannot summon the invisible by some magical process. All that can be done is to stimulate thought and assume that the audience will inwardly energize their thinking into following what can only be indicated by the words. Yet nowadays it will frequently happen that many of the listeners—I do not, of course, refer to those who are sitting in this hall—begin to yawn, because they imagine that thinking ought to be passive, and then they fall asleep because they are not following the subject actively. People like everything to be demonstrated to the eye, illustrated by means of lantern-slides or the like, so that it is unnecessary to think at all. Indeed, they cannot think. That was the beginning, and it has gone still further. In a performance of "Hamlet," for instance, one must accompany the business, and also the spoken word, in order to understand it. But to-day the drama is deserted for the cinema, where one need not exert oneself in any way; the pictures roll off the machine and can be watched quite inertly. And so man's own inner activity of thought has gradually been lost. But it is this which must be taken hold of. Then it will be perceived that thinking is not simply something which can be stimulated from outside, but represents an inward force within the being of man himself.

The kind of thinking current in our modern civilization is only one aspect of this force of thought. If we inwardly observe it, from the other side as it were, it is revealed as the force that builds up the human being from childhood. Before this can be understood, the inner, plastic force that transforms abstract thought into pictures must come into play. Then, after the necessary efforts have been made, we reach the stage I have called in my book the beginning of meditation. At this point we not only begin to lead ability over into art, but thought is raised into Imagination. We stand in a world of Imagination, knowing that it is not a creation of our own fantasy, but an actual, objective world. We are fully conscious that although we do not as yet possess this objective world itself in the imaginative picture, we have the pictoriality of it. And now the only point is also to realize that we must get beyond the picture.

Much has to be done if we would come to this inner creative thinking, to this thinking that does not merely contain pictures of fantasy, but pictures bearing their own reality within them. Next, however, we must again be able to eliminate the whole of this creative activity: we must accomplish a first, inwardly moral act. For this indeed constitutes a moral action within the inner being of man: when one has taken all the trouble to achieve this pictorial-active thinking (and you can read in my book how much trouble must be taken), when all the forces of soul have been applied and the powers of the self exerted to their very utmost, then after this utmost exertion one must be able to eliminate once more what has been won in this way. In his own being man must have developed the highest fruits of this thinking that has been raised to the level of meditation, and then be capable of selflessness. He must be able to eliminate all that has been thus acquired. This is different from not having anything, not having won anything in the first place. And now if he has first of all made every effort to strengthen the self in this way, and then destroys the results of this once more through his own powers so that his consciousness becomes empty, there surges into his human consciousness a spiritual world; the spiritual world enters the being of man. Then it is seen that for knowledge of the spiritual world spiritual forces of cognition are required. Active picture-thinking may be called *Imagination*. When the spiritual world pours into the consciousness that has in turn been emptied by dint of the greatest conceivable efforts, it does so by way of what may be called *Inspiration*. Having gone through Imagination, we can make ourselves worthy through the moral act just described to grasp the spiritual world lying behind outer nature and man.

I will now endeavour to show you how from this point we are led over to religion.

Let me draw your attention to the following: Inasmuch as Anthroposophy strives for true Imagination, it leads not only to knowledge or to art that in itself is of the nature of a picture, but to the spiritual reality contained in the picture. Anthroposophy bridges the gulf between knowledge and art in such a way that at a higher level, suited to modern life and the present age, the unity of science and art which humanity has abandoned can enter civilization once again. This unity must be re-attained, for the schism between science and art has disrupted the very being of man. To pass from the state of disruption to unity and inner harmony—it is for this above all that modern man must strive.

Thus far I have spoken of the harmony between science and art. In the third part of the lecture I will develop the subject further, in connection with religion and morality.

· · · · · · ·

Knowledge that thus draws the creative activity of the universe into itself can flow directly into art, and this same path from knowledge to art can be extended and continued. It was so continued through the powers of the old imaginative knowledge, which also found the way, without any intervening cleft, into the life of religion. He who applied himself to this kind of knowledge—primitive and instinctive though it was in early humanity—did not feel it as something external, for in his knowing and thinking he felt that the divinity of the world lived in him, that the creatively Divine passed over into the artistic creativeness of man. Then the way could be found, however, to raise what man in art impressed on matter to a still higher consecration. The activity which he made his own as he embodied the Divine-Spiritual in outer material substance he could then extend into acts wherein he was fully conscious that he, as man, was expressing the will of the divine powers of the world. He felt himself pervaded by divine creative power, and as the path was followed from the elaboration of material substance to human action, art passed over, by way of ritual, into the service of the divine. Artistic creation became service of God. What is done in the cult represents the consecrated artistic deeds of ancient humanity. Artistic deed was raised into cultic deed, the glorifying of God through matter to devotion to God through the service of the cult. And as man thus bridged the gulf between art and religion there arose a religion in full harmony with knowledge and with art. Albeit primitive and instinctive, this knowledge was none the less a true picture, and as such it could lead human deeds to become, in the acts of ritual, a direct portrayal of the Divine.

In this way the transition from art to religion was made possible. Is it still possible with our present-day mode of knowledge? The ancient clairvoyant perception had revealed to man pictorially the spiritual in every creature and process of nature, and through the surrender and devotion of man to the spirit within the nature-processes, the all-swaying, all-creative spirituality of the cosmos passed over into the cult.

How do we know the world to-day? Once more, to describe is better than criticism, for as the following lectures will show, the development of our present mode of knowledge was a necessity in the history of mankind. To-day I am merely placing certain suggestive thoughts before you. We have gradually lost our once spiritual insight into the being and processes of nature. We take pride in eliminating the spirit in our observation of nature, and finally reach such hypothetical conceptions as attribute the origin of our planet to the movements of a primeval nebula. Mechanical stirrings in this nebula are said to be the origin of all the kingdoms of nature, even so far as man. And according to these same laws—which loom so large in our whole would-be objective mode of thinking, this earth must finally end through the so-called warmth-death. All ideals achieved by man, having proceeded as a kind of Fata Morgana out of nature, will disappear, until at the end there will remain only the tomb of earthly existence.

If this line of thought is recognized as true by science and men are honest and brave enough to face its inevitable consequences, they cannot but admit that all religious and moral life is also a Fata Morgana and must so remain! Yet the human being cannot endure this thought, and so must hold fast to the remnants of olden times, when religion and morality had achieved a harmony with knowledge and with art. Religion and morality to-day do not spring creatively out of man's inner being: they rest on tradition and are a heritage from ages when all things revealed themselves through the instinctive life of man, when God—and the moral world with Him—were alike made manifest. Our strivings for knowledge to-day can reveal neither God nor a moral world. Science attains to the end of the animal species: man is cast out. Honest inner thinking can find no bridge over the gulf fixed between knowledge and the religious life.

All true religions have sprung from Inspiration. True, the early form of Inspiration was not so conscious as that to which we must now attain, yet it was there instinctively, and rightly do the religions trace their origin back to it. Such faiths as will no longer recognize living inspiration and revelation from the spirit in the immediate present will have to be content with tradition. But such faiths lack all inner vitality, all direct motive-power of religious life. This motive-power and vitality must be re-won, for only so can our social organism be healed.

I have shown how man must regain a knowledge that passes by way of art to Imagination and thence to Inspiration. If he re-acquires all that flows down from the inspirations of a spiritual world into human consciousness, true religion will once again appear. And then intellectual discussion about the nature of Christ will cease, for once again it will be known—as it can indeed be known through Inspiration—that the Christ was the human bearer of an actual Divine Being Who had descended from spiritual worlds into earthly existence. Without supersensible knowledge there can be no understanding of the Christ. If Christianity is again to be deeply rooted in humanity, the path to supersensible knowledge must be rediscovered. Inspiration must again impart a truly religious life to mankind in order that knowledge—derived no longer merely from the external observation of nature—may find no abyss dividing it alike from art and religion. Knowledge, art, religion—these three will then be in harmony.

Primeval man counted on the presence of God in human deeds when he made his art a divine office, and when he shared in the fire that can glow in the heart of man when the divine will pervades the acts of ritual. And when the path from outer, objective knowledge to Inspiration is found once again, religion will flow directly from Inspiration and modern man will be able—as was primeval man—to stand within a God-given morality. In those ancient days man felt: " If I have the cult, if I have the divine service, if the cult is in the world and I am woven into it, then my inner being is filled so that in the whole of my life and not only where the cult is celebrated I can make God present in the world."

To be able to make God present in the world—this is true morality. Nature cannot lead man to morality. Only that which lifts him above nature, filling him with the Divine-Spiritual—this alone can lead man to morality. Only that intuition which comes over man, when through the religious life he places himself in the spirit, can fill him with real inmost morality at once human and divine. The attainment of Inspiration thus rebuilds the bridge once existing instinctively in human civilization between religion and morality. As knowledge leads upwards through art to the heights of supersensible life, so, through religious worship, spiritual heights are brought down to earthly existence, so that we can fill this existence with the impulse of an essential, primal, direct morality actually experienced by man. Thus will man himself become in truth the individual bearer of a life pulsed through by morality, filled with an immediate moral impulse. Morality will then be a creation of the individual himself, and the last abyss between religion and morality will be bridged. The intuition in which primitive man stood as he enacted his ritual will be re-created in a new form, and a morality truly corresponding with modern conditions will arise from a modern religious life. We need this for the renewal of our civilization. We need it in order that what to-day is mere heritage, mere tradition, may spring again into original life. This primordial impulse is necessary for our complicated social life that is threatening to spread chaos through the world. We need a harmony between knowledge, art, religion, and morality. In a new form we need this way which leads from the earth and along which we win our knowledge, passing through Inspiration and through the arts to the direct life in the supersensible, to a taking hold of the supersensible, so that we can again lead down into social life on the earth the supersensible which we have felt in religion and transformed into will. Only when we see the social question as one of morality and religion can we grapple with it in its full depths, and this we cannot do until the moral and religious life arises from spiritual knowledge. If man again achieves spiritual knowledge, he will be able to do what is needed, to link his further evolution to an instinctive origin. He will find what must be found for the healing of humanity: harmony between science, art, religion and morality.

II

Principles of Greek Education

That the subject of education is exercising the minds and souls of all men at the present day is not to be questioned. It is everywhere apparent. If, then, an art of education is advocated here which is derived directly from spiritual life and spiritual perception, it is its inner nature rather than the urgency of its outward appeal which differentiates it from the reforms generally demanded to-day.

There is a general feeling nowadays that the conditions of civilization are in rapid transition, and for the sake of the organization of our social life we must pay heed to the many new changes and developments of modern times. Already there is a feeling—a feeling which only a short time ago was rarely present—that the child of to-day is a very different being from the child of a recent past, and that it is much more difficult nowadays for age to come to an understanding with youth than was the case in earlier times.

The art of education, however, of which I have here to speak, is concerned rather with the inner development of human civilization. It is concerned with what has changed the souls of men in the course of ages, with the evolution through which, in the course of hundreds, nay, even thousands of years, these souls have passed. The attempt will be made to explore the means by which, in this particular age, we may reach the being of man as it lives in the child. It is generally admitted that the successive periods of time in nature can be differentiated. We need only think of the way in which man takes these differentiations into account in daily life. Take the example nearest to hand—the day itself. Our relation to the processes of nature is quite different in the morning, at noon, and at night, and we should think it absurd to ignore the course of the day. We should also think it absurd not to pay due heed, however, to the development revealed in human life itself—to ignore, for instance, the fact that an old man's needs are different from those of a child. In the case of nature we respect this fact of development. But man has not yet accustomed himself to respect the fact of the general evolution of humanity. We do not take account of the fact that centuries ago there lived a humanity very different from the humanity of the Middle Ages or of the present time. We must learn to know the nature of the inner forces of human beings, if our treatment of children at the present time is to be practical and not merely theoretical. We must investigate from within those forces in man which hold sway in this present day.

The principles of Waldorf School education—as it may be called—are, therefore, in no sense revolutionary. In Waldorf School education there is full recognition of all that is great and worthy of esteem in the brilliant achievements of educationists of all countries during the nineteenth century. There is no desire to cast everything aside and imagine that the only possible thing is something radically new. The aim is rather to investigate the inner forces now ruling in the nature of man in order to be able to take them into account in education, and thereby to find a true place in social life for the human being in body, soul, and spirit. For—as we shall see in the course of these lectures—education has always been a concern of social life, and still is so at the present time. It must be a social concern in the future as well. In education, therefore, there must be an understanding of the social demands of any given epoch. To begin with, I want to describe to you in three stages the development of the nature of education in Western civilization. The best way will be to consider the educational ideals of the different epochs—the ideals striven for by those who desired to rise to the highest stage of human existence, to the stage from which they could render the most useful service to their fellow-men. It will be well in such a study to go back to the earliest of those past ages which we feel to survive as a cultural influence even at the present time. Nobody to-day will dispute the still living influence in all human aims and aspirations of the Greek civilization, and the question, " In what way did the Greek seek to raise the human being to a certain stage of perfection ? " must be of fundamental significance to the educator. We must therefore consider the progress of successive epochs in respect of the perfecting, of the educating and instructing of the human being.

Let us see, to begin with—and, indeed, we shall have to study this question in detail—what was the Greek ideal for the teacher, that is to say, for the man who desired not only to develop to the highest stage of humanity for his own sake, but for the sake of being able to guide others along their path. What was the Greek ideal of education ? The Greek ideal of education was the Gymnast, that is to say, one who had completely harmonized his bodily nature and, to the extent that was thought necessary in those days, all the qualities of his soul and spirit. A man able to bring the divine beauty of the world to expression in the beauty of his own body, able to bring the divine beauty of the world into bodily expression in the child, in the boy—this was the Gymnast, the man by whom Greek civilization was upborne.

It is easy, from a kind of modern superiority, to look down upon the Gymnast's manner of education, based as it was on the bodily nature of man. But there exists a total misunderstanding of what was meant in Greece by the word Gymnast. If, nevertheless, we do still admire Greek civilization and culture to-day, if we still regard it as the ideal of highest development to be permeated with Greek culture, it will be well to remember while we do this, that the Greek himself was not primarily concerned with the development of so-called spirituality in the human being. He was only concerned to develop the human body in such a way that, as a result of the harmony of its parts and its modes of activity, the body itself should blossom into a manifestation of divine beauty. The Greek confidently expected of the body just what we expect of the plant: that it will of itself unfold into blossom under the influence of sunlight and warmth, if the root has received the proper kind of treatment. And in our devotion to Greek culture to-day we must not forget that the bearer of this culture was the Gymnast, one who had not taken the third step first, so to speak, but the first step first: the harmonization of the bodily nature of man. All the beauty, all the greatness, all the perfection of Greek culture was not directly sought, but was regarded as growing naturally out of the beautiful, harmonious, powerful body, by virtue of the inner nature and activity of earthly man. Our understanding of Greek civilization, especially of Greek education, will be one-sided unless our admiration for the spiritual greatness of Greece is linked with the knowledge that the Gymnast was the ideal of Greek education.

Then, as we follow the continuous development of humanity, we come to a most significant incision in the transition from Greek to Roman culture. In Roman civilization we see, to begin with, the emergence of that cultivation of abstractions which later led to the separation of spirit, soul, and body, and placed a special emphasis on this three-fold division. We can see how the principle of beauty in Greek " gymnastic " education was indeed imitated in Roman culture, but how, nevertheless, the education of body and soul fell into two separate spheres. The Roman still set great store by the training of the body, but little by little—and almost imperceptibly—this fell into a secondary place. The attention was directed more to something that was considered more important in human nature—the element of soul. The training which in Greece was bound up with the ideal of the Gymnast, gradually changes, in Roman culture, into a training of the soul qualities.

This continues on through the Middle Ages—an epoch when the qualities of soul were considered to be of a higher order than those of the body. And from this Romanized human nature, as we may call it, there arises another ideal of education. Early in the Middle Ages there appears an educational ideal for the highest classes of men, which was a fruit of Roman civilization. It was in its essence a culture of the soul—of the soul, that is, in so far as it reveals itself outwardly in man.

The Gymnast was gradually superseded by another type of human being. To-day we no longer have any strong, historical consciousness of this change, but those who study the Middle Ages intimately will realize that it did actually take place. The ideal of education was no longer the Gymnast, but the Rhetorician, one whose main training was the training of speech, that is to say, of something that is essentially a quality of soul. How the human being can work through speech, as a Rhetorician—this was an outcome of Roman culture carried over into the first period of the Middle Ages. It represents the change from an education adapted purely to the body to an education more particularly of the soul, one which carries on the training of the body as a secondary activity. And because the Middle Ages made use of the Rhetorician for spreading the spiritual life as it was cultivated in the monastic schools and elsewhere in medieval education, it came about, though the name was not always used, that the Rhetorician assumed in the sphere of education the place which had once been held by the Greek Gymnast. Thus, in reviewing the ideals which have been regarded as the highest expression of man, we see how humanity advances from the educational ideal of Gymnast to that of the Rhetorician.

Now this had its effect upon the methods of education. The education of children was brought into line with what was held to be the ideal of human perfection. And one who can observe historically will perceive that even the usages of our modern education, the manner in which language and speech are taught to children, are a heritage from the practice of the Middle Ages which had the Rhetorician as educational ideal.

Then came the middle of the Middle Ages, with its great swing over to the intellectual, with all the honour and respect which it paid to the things of the intellect. A new educational ideal of human development arose—an ideal which represents exactly the opposite of the Greek ideal. It was an ideal which gave the highest place to the intellectual and spiritual development of man. He who knows something —the knower—he now became the ideal. Whereas throughout the whole of the Middle Ages he who could do something, do something with the powers of his soul, who could convince others, remained the ideal of education, now the knower becomes the ideal. We have only to look at the earliest university institutions, at the University of Paris, for example in the Middle Ages, to realize that the ideal there is not yet the knower, but the doer, the man who can convince most through speech, who is the most skilful in argument, the master of dialectic—of the word which now takes on the colour of thought. We still find the Rhetorician as the ideal of education, though the Rhetorician himself is tinged with the hue of thought.

And now, with modern civilization, another ideal arises for evolving man—an ideal which is again reflected in the education of the child. Our own education of children, even in this age of materialism, has remained under the influence of this ideal right down to the present time. Now for the first time there arises the ideal of the Doctor, the Professor. The Doctor becomes the ideal for the perfect human being.

Thus we see the three stages in human evolution: the Gymnast, the Rhetorician, the Doctor. The Gymnast is one who can handle the whole human organism from out of what he regards as the divine ordering and working in the world, in the cosmos. The Rhetorician only knows how to handle the soul-nature in so far as it manifests in the bodily nature. The Gymnast trains the body, and through it, the soul and spirit, to the heights of Greek civilization. The Rhetorician is concerned with the soul, and attains his crown and his glory as the orator of the things of the soul, as the Church orator. And lastly, we see how skill, the ability to do, ceases to be valued. The man who only knows, the man, that is, who no longer handles the soul-nature in its bodily working, but only that which reigns invisibly in the inner being—the man who only knows now stands as the ideal of the highest stage of education. This, however, reflects itself into the most elementary principles of education. For it was the Gymnasts in Greece who also educated the children. It was the Rhetoricians, later on, who educated the children. Finally, in more modern times, just when materialism arose in civilization as a whole, it was the Doctor who educated the children. Thus bodily, gymnastic education develops into rhetorical soul-education, and this in turn develops into doctorial education. Our modern education is the outcome of the doctorial ideal. And those who desire to seek, in the deepest principles of modern education, those things which really ought to be understood, must carefully observe what has been introduced as a result of this doctorial ideal.

Side by side with this, however, a new ideal has emerged into greater and greater prominence in the modern age. It is the ideal of the " universal human." Men had eyes and ears only for what belonged by right to the Doctor, and the longing arose once again to educate the whole human being, to add to the doctorial education, which was even being crammed into the tiny child (for the Doctors wrote the text books, thought out the methods of teachings), to add to this, the education of the universal human. And to-day, those who judge from a fundamental, elementary feeling for human nature, want to have their say in educational matters.

Thus for inner reasons the problem of education to-day has become a problem of the times. We must bear this inner course of human evolution in mind if we would understand the present age, for a true development of education must tend to nothing less than a superseding of this " Doctor " principle. If I were briefly to summarize one particular aspect of the aim of Waldorf School education, I should say —to-day, of course, merely in a preliminary sense—that we are trying to turn this " doctorial " education into a human education of man as a whole.

. . . .

Now we cannot understand the essential nature of the education which had its rise in Greek civilization and has continued in its further development on into our own times, unless we look at the course of human evolution from the days of Greek civilization to our own in the right light. Greek civilization was really a continuation, an offshoot, as it were, of Oriental civilization. All that had developed in the evolution of humanity for thousands of years over in Asia, in the East, found its final expression in Greece, especially, I believe, in Greek education. Not till then did there come an important incision in evolution: the transition to Roman culture. Roman culture is the source of all that later flowed into the whole of Western civilization—even as far as America.

Hence it is impossible to understand the essential nature of Greek education unless we have a true conception of the whole character of Oriental development. To one who stood by the cradle of the civilization out of which arose the wonderful Vedas and the Vedanta, it would have seemed the purest nonsense to imagine that the highest development of human nature is to be attained by sitting with books in front of one in order to get through examinations. And to imagine that anyone could become a perfected human being after having literally maltreated (for "trained" is not the word) for years, if the man be industrious, for months, if he be lazy, an indefinite something that goes by the name of the "human spirit," in order then to be questioned by someone as to how much he knows—all this, as I say, would have seemed the purest nonsense to a man who stood at the cradle of Oriental civilization. We do not understand the development of human civilization unless we sometimes pause to consider how the ideal of one epoch appears to the eyes of another. For what steps were taken by a man of the ancient East who desired to acquire the sublime culture offered to his people in the age preceding that of the inspiration behind the Vedas? What he practised was fundamentally a kind of bodily culture. And he hoped, as the result of a special cult of the body—one-sided though this would appear to-day—to attain to the crowning glory of human life, to the loftiest spirituality—if this lay within his destiny. Hence an exceedingly delicate culture of the body was the method adopted in the highest education of the ancient East—not the reading of books and the maltreatment of an abstract " spirit." I will give you an example of this refined bodily culture. It consisted in a definite and vigorously systematic regulation of the breathing. When man breathes—as indeed he must do in order to provide himself with the proper supply of oxygen from minute to minute—the process is an unconscious one. He carries out the whole breathing process unconsciously. The ancient oriental made this breathing process—which is fundamentally a bodily function—into something which was carried out with consciousness. He drew in his breath in accordance with a definite law, held it back and breathed it out again according to a definite law. While doing this he arranged his body in a quite definite way. The legs and arms must be held in certain positions; that is to say, the path of the breath through the physical organism when it reached the knee, for instance, must bend round into the horizontal direction. And so the ancient oriental who was seeking to reach the stage of human perfection sat with legs crossed beneath him. The man who wished to experience the revelation of the spirit in himself must achieve it as the result of a training of the body, a training directed in particular to the air-processes in the human being, but centred, nevertheless, in the bodily nature.

Now what lies at the basis of this kind of training and education ? The flower and fruit of a plant live within the root and if the root receives proper care, both flower and fruit must develop properly under the light and warmth of the sun. In the same way, the soul and spirit live in the bodily nature of man, in the body that is created by God. If a man then takes hold of the roots in the body, knowing that Divinity lives within them, develops these bodily roots in the right way and then gives himself up to the life that is freely unfolding, the soul and spirit within the roots develop like the inner forces of the plant that pour out of the root and unfold under the light and warmth of the sun.

Any abstract development of spirit would have seemed to

the oriental just as if we were to shut off our plants from the sunlight, perhaps put them into a cellar and then make them grow under electric light, because we did not consider the free light of the sun good enough for them. The fact that the oriental only looked to the bodily nature was deeply rooted in his whole conception of humanity. This bodily development afterwards, of course, became one-sided—had already become so in the Jewish culture—but the very one-sideness shows us that the universal view was: body, soul, and spirit are one. Here, on earth, between birth and death, the soul and spirit must be sought for in the body.

It may possibly cause some astonishment to see the ancient spiritual culture of the East in this light, but when we study the true course of human evolution we shall find that the loftiest achievements of civilization were attained in times when man was still able to behold the soul and spirit wholly within the body. This was a development of the very greatest significance for the innermost being of human civilization. Now why was the oriental—for it must be remembered that his whole concern was a quest for the spirit—why was the oriental justified in striving for the spirit by methods that were really based upon the bodily nature of man ? He was justified because his philosophy did not merely open his eyes to the earthly but also to the supersensible. And he knew: To regard the soul and spirit here on earth as being independent, is to see them (forgive this rather trivial analogy, but in the sense of oriental wisdom it is absolutely correct) in the form of a " plucked hen," not a hen with feathers and therefore not a complete hen. The idea we have of the soul and spirit would have seemed to the oriental analogous to a hen with its feathers plucked, for he knew the soul and spirit, he knew the reality of what we seek in other worlds. He had a concrete supersensible perception of it. He felt justified in seeking earthly man in his material, bodily revelation, because his fundamental conviction was that in other worlds, the plucked hen, the naked soul, is again endowed with spiritual feathers when it reaches the proper place.

Thus it was the very spiritual nature of his conception of

the world that prompted the oriental, in considering the earthly evolution of the human being, to bear in mind before all else that within the body when man is born, when he comes forth as a purely physical being, resting within the physical body of the little child in a most wonderful way there is soul and spirit. For the oriental knew that when this *Physis* is handled in the truly spiritual way, soul and spirit will proceed from it. This was the keynote for the education, even of the Sage, in the East. It was a conviction which passed over into Greek culture, for Greek culture is an offshoot of oriental civilisation. And now we understand why it was that the Greeks—who brought the conviction of the East to its uttermost expression—adopted, even in the case of the young, their own particular kind of training of the human being. It was the result of oriental influence. The particular attention paid to the bodily nature in Greek civilization simply represents what the Greek became as a result of colonization from the East and from Egypt—whence his whole mode of existence was derived.

When we look at the Greek palestras where the Gymnasts worked, we must see in their activities a continuation of the development which the East—from a profoundly spiritual conception of the world—strove for in the man who was to reach the highest ideal of human perfection on earth. The oriental would never have considered a one-sided development of soul or spirit to be the ideal of human perfection. The learning and instruction that has become the ideal of later times, would have seemed to him a deadening of what the Gods had given to man for his life on earth. And, fundamentally, this was still the conception of the Greek.

It is a strange experience to realize how the spiritual culture of Greece—which we to-day think of as so sublime—was regarded in those times by non-Greek peoples. An historical anecdote, handed down by tradition, tells us that a barbarian prince once went to Greece, visited the places where education was being carried on and had a conversation with one of the most famous Gymnasts. The barbarian prince said: "I cannot understand these insane practices of yours! First you rub the young men with oil—the symbol of peace—then you strew sand over them, just as if they were being prepared for some peaceful ceremony, and then they begin to hurl themselves about as if they were mad, seizing hold of and jumping at each other. One throws the other down or punches his chin so vigorously that his shoulders have to be well shaken to prevent him from suffocating. I simply do not understand such a display, and it can be of no conceivable use to the human being." This was what the barbarian prince said to the Greek. But in spite of this, the spiritual glory of Greece was derived from what the barbarian prince thought to be so much barbarism. And just as the Greek Gymnast only smiled at the barbarian who did not understand how the body must be trained in order to make the spirit manifest, so would a Greek, if he could rise again and see our customary methods of teaching and education (which really date from earlier times), laugh within himself at the barbarism that has developed since the days of Greece and speaks of an abstract soul and spirit. The Greek in his turn would say: "This is analogous to a plucked hen. You have taken man's feathers away from him!" The Greek would have thought it barbaric that the boys should not wrestle and fall upon one another in the manner described. The barbarian prince, however, could see no meaning or purpose in Greek education. Thus by studying the course of human development and observing what was held to be of value in other epochs, we may acquire a foundation whence we can also come to a right valuation of things in our own time.

. . . .

Let us now turn our attention to those places where the Greek Gymnast educated and taught the youths who were entrusted to him in the seventh year of life. What we find there naturally differs essentially from the kind of national educational ideal, for instance, that held sway in the nineteenth century. In this connection, what I shall say does not merely hold good for this or that particular nation, but for all civilized nations. What we behold when we turn our attention to one of these places in Greece where the young were educated from the seventh year of life onwards, can, if it is rightly permeated with modern impulses, afford us a true basis for understanding what is necessary for education and instruction to-day. The youths were trained—and the word 'trained' is here always used in its very highest sense—on the one hand in Orchestric and on the other in Palestric. Orchestric, to the outer eye, was entirely a bodily exercise, a kind of concerted dance, but arranged in a very special way. It was a dance with a most complicated form. The boys learnt to move in a definite form in accordance with measure, beat, rhythm, and altogether in accordance with a certain plastic-musical principle. The boy, moving in this choral dance, felt a kind of inner soul-warmth pouring through all his limbs and co-ordinating them. This experience was at the same time perceived by the spectators as a beautifully composed musical dance. The whole thing was a revelation of the beauty of the Godhead and at the same time an experience of this beauty in the inner being of man. All that was experienced through this orchestric was felt and sensed inwardly. And through being felt and sensed inwardly it was transformed as physical, bodily process into something expressive of the soul, inspiring the hand to play the zither, inspiring speech and word to become song. To understand song and the playing of the zither in ancient Greece we must see them as blossoming out of the choral dance. Out of what he experienced in the dance, man was inspired to set the strings in movement so that he might hear the sound arising from the choral dance. From his own movement he experienced some thing that poured into his word—and his word became song.

Gymnastic and musical culture—this held sway throughout the education given in the Greek palestra. But the musical and soul qualities thus acquired were born from the outer bodily movements which in wonderful lawfulness of form were made in the dances in the palestra. And if to-day one penetrates with direct perception to the meaning of these ordered movements in a Greek palestra—which the barbarian prince could not understand—one finds that all the forms of movement, all the movements of the individual human being, were most wonderfully arranged so that the direct result was not at first the musical element that I have already described —but something else. When we study the measures and the rhythms that were mysteriously interwoven into orchestric, into the choral dance, we find that nothing could have a more healing, health-giving effect upon the breathing system and the blood circulation of man than these bodily exercises which were carried out in the Greek choral dances. If the question were put: When does man out of himself breathe in the best way? How does man best bring his blood into movement by means of the breathing?—the answer would have been that the boy must move, must carry out dance-like movements from his seventh year onwards. Then—as they said in those times—his systems of breathing and blood circulation rest not on decadence but on healing. The aim of all this orchestric was to express the systems of breathing and blood circulation in the human being in the most perfect way. For the conviction was that when the blood circulation is functioning properly it works right down to the very finger tips, and then instinctively the human being will strike the strings of the zither or the strings of the lute in the right way. This was, as it were, the flower of the blood circulation. The whole rhythmic system of the human being was kindled in the right way through the choral dance.

As a result of this, it was expected that a musical, spiritual quality would develop in the playing, for it was known that when the individual human being carries out the corresponding movements with his limbs in the choral dance, the breathing system is so inspired that it quite naturally functions in a spiritual way. And the final consequence is that the breath will overflow into what the human being expresses outwardly through the larynx and its related organs. It was known that the healing effects of the choral dance on the breathing system would enkindle song. And thus the crowning climax, zither-playing and song, was drawn from the healthy organism trained in the right way through the choral dance. The physical nature, the soul and the spirit—these were looked upon as an inner unity, an inner totality in earthly man. And this was the whole spirit of Greek education.

And now let us look at what was developed in palestric—which gave its name to the places of education in Greece because it was the common property, so to speak, of the educated people. What was it, we ask, that was studied in those forms, in which, for instance, wrestling was evolved? And we see that the whole system existed for the purpose of unfolding two qualities in the human being. The will, stimulated by bodily movement, grew strong and forceful in two directions. All movement and all palestric in wrestling was intended to bring suppleness, skill and mobility, purposeful mobility, into the limbs of the wrestler. Man's whole system of movement was to be harmonized in such a way that the separate parts should work together properly and that for any particular mood of his soul he should be able to make the appropriate movements with skill, controlling his limbs from within. The rounding of the movements into purposeful life—this was one side of palestric. The other side was the radial of the movement, as it were, where force must flow into the movement. Skill on the one side, force on the other. The power to hold out against and overcome the forces working in opposition, to be strong oneself in order to experience something in the world—this was the other side. Skill, proficiency, and harmonization of the different parts of the organism, and, on the other hand, the development of power; the ability freely to radiate and express his own being everywhere in the world—this was the other side.

It was held that when the human being thus harmonized his system of movement through palestric, he entered into true relationship with the cosmos. The arms, legs and the breathing as developed by palestric were then given over to the activities of the human being in the world, for it was known that when the arm is rightly developed through palestric it links itself with the stream of cosmic forces which in turn flow to the human brain and then, from out of the cosmos, reveal the great ideas to man. Just as the musical element was not expected to arise out of a special musical training, but simply united—in most cases about the age of twenty—with what was drawn out of the blood circulation and the breathing, so what had to be learnt, for example, as mathematics and geometry united with the bodily culture in palestric. It was known that geometry is inspired in the human being by right movements of the arms.

To-day people do not learn of these things from history, for they have been entirely forgotten. What I have told you is, nevertheless, the truth, and it justifies the Greeks in having placed the Gymnasts at the head of their educational institutions. For the Gymnast best succeeded in bringing about the spiritual development of the Greeks by giving them freedom. He did not cram their brains or try to make them into walking encyclopedias, but placed the best qualified organs of the human being into the cosmos in the right way. Then man became receptive for the spiritual world. Like the man of the East the Greek Gymnast was convinced that this happened, only in a later form.

What I have really done to-day, by giving an introductory description of an ancient method of education, is to put a question before you. And I have done so because we must probe very deeply if we are to discover the true principles of education in our time. It is absolutely necessary to enter into these depths of human evolution in order to discover, in these depths, the right way to formulate the questions which will help us to solve the problem of our own education and methods of instruction. To-day, therefore, I wanted to place before you one aspect of the subject we are considering. As we proceed, the lectures are intended to give a more detailed answer—an answer suited to the requirements of the present age—to the question which has been raised to-day and will be developed to-morrow.

Our mode of study, therefore, must be the outcome of a true understanding of the great problem of education raised by the evolutionary course of humanity, and we must then pass on to the answers that may be given by a knowledge of the nature and constitution of the human being at the present time.

III

Greek Education and the Middle Ages

When I attempted to bring before you the Greek ideal of education, it could only be with the object of stimulating by means of this ideal those ideas which must prevail in our modern system of education. For at the present stage of human life it is, of course, impossible to adopt the same educational methods as the Greeks. In spite of this, however, an all-embracing truth in regard to education can, above all, be learnt from the Greek ideal, and to begin with we must place this truth before us as it was affirmed in the culture of ancient Greece.

Up to the seventh year of life, the Greek child was brought up at home. Public education was concerned with children only after the age of seven. They were brought up at home, where the women lived in seclusion, apart from the ordinary pursuits of social life, which were an affair of the men. This in itself confirms a truth of education, without knowledge of which one cannot really educate or teach, for the seventh year of life is an all-important period of childhood.

The main phenomenon characteristic of the seventh year of human life is the change of teeth. This is an event to which far too little importance is attached nowadays. For think of it—the nature of the human organism is such that it brings the first teeth with it, as an inheritance, or, rather, it brings with it the force to produce these first teeth out of the organism which are worn out by the seventh year. It is absolutely incorrect to imagine that the force which pushes up the second teeth at about the seventh year unfolds for the first time at this age. It is developing slowly from birth onwards, and simply reaches its culmination about the seventh year of life. Then it brings forth the second teeth from the totality of force in the human organization. This event is of the most extraordinary importance in the course of human life as a whole, because it does not occur again. The forces present between birth and the seventh year reach their culmination with the appearance of the second teeth, and they do not act again in all the course of earthly life. Now this fact must be properly understood, but it can only be understood by an unprejudiced observation of other processes that are being enacted in the human being at about this seventh year of life. Up to the seventh year the human being grows and develops according to nature-principles, as it were. The nature-forces of growth, the being of the soul and the spiritual sphere have not yet separated from one another in the child's total organization; they form a unity up to the seventh year. While the human being is developing his organs, his nervous system and his blood circulation, this development betokens also the evolution of his soul and spirit. The human being is provided with the strong inner impulsive force which brings forth the second teeth, because everything in this period of life is still interwoven. With the coming of the second teeth, this impelling force weakens. It holds back somewhat; it does not work so strongly from out of the inner being. Why is this? Now suppose we were to get new teeth every seven years. (I will take an extreme illustration for the sake of clarity.) If the same organic forces which we bear within us up to the seventh year, if this unity formed by body, soul, and spirit were to continue through the whole of life, new teeth would appear approximately every seven years! The old teeth would fall out and be replaced by new ones, but throughout our whole life we should remain children as we are up to the seventh year. We should not unfold the life of soul and spirit that is separated off from the nature-life. The fact that the physical impelling force decreases in the seventh year and the body in a certain sense no longer thrives and flourishes so well—for the body now produces weaker, more delicate forces from itself—makes it possible for the subtler forces of soul life to develop. The body grows weaker, the soul stronger, as it were.

A similar process also takes place at puberty, in the fourteenth or fifteenth year. The element of soul now weakens to a certain extent and the spiritual functions make their appearance. So that if we take the course of the first three life-periods, up till the seventh year man is paramountly a being of body-soul-spirit in one; from the seventh to the fourteenth years he is a being of body and soul with a separate nature of soul and spirit; and from puberty onwards he is a threefold being—a physical being, a being of soul and a being of spirit.

This truth opens up deep vistas into the whole evolution of the human being. Indeed, unless we appreciate it we really ought not to venture upon the education of children. For unless we realize the far-reaching consequences of this truth, all education must really be more or less a dilettante affair.

The Greek—and this is the amazing thing—knew of this truth. To the Greek, it was a quite unshakeable law that when a boy had reached his seventh year he must be taken away from his parents' house, from the mere nature-principles, the elementary matter-of-course upbringing. This knowledge was so deeply rooted in the Greeks that we do well to remind ourselves of it to-day. Later on, in the Middle Ages, traces of this all-important principle of education still existed.

The modern age of rationalism and intellectualism has forgotten all these things, and, indeed, even takes pride in showing that it places no value on such truth, for the child is usually required to go to school at an earlier age, a year or even more before the end of the seventh year. We may say, indeed, this departure from such eternal principles of human evolution is just typical of the chaos obtaining in our modern system of education, out of which we must extricate, we must work ourselves. The Greek placed so high a value on this truth that he based all education upon it; for what I described to you yesterday all happened in order to regulate education in its light.

What did the Greek see in the little child from birth to the time of the change of teeth? A being sent down to earth from spiritual heights! He saw in man a being who had lived in a spiritual world before earthly life. And as he observed the child he tried to discover whether its body was rightly expressing the divine life of pre-earthly existence. It was of importance for the Greek that in the child up to the seventh year he should recognize that a physical body is here enclosing a spiritual being who has descended. There was a terribly barbaric custom in certain regions of Greece to expose and thus kill those children who were instinctively believed to be only sheaths, not expressing a true spiritual being in their physical nature. This was the outcome of rigid regard to the thought that the physical human being in the first seven years of life is the vesture of a divine-spiritual being.

Now when the child passes its seventh year—and this, too, was known in Greece—it descends a second stage lower. During the first seven years the child is in a certain sense released from the heavens, still bearing its own inherited sheath, which is laid aside at the seventh year, for not only the first teeth but the whole body is cast off every seven years and so cast off for the first time in the seventh year. In the first seven years of life this bodily sheath revealed to the Greek what the forces of pre-earthly life had made out of the child. The child bears its earthly sheath proper, its very first earthly sheath, only from about the seventh to the fourteenth years onwards.

I am trying now to express these things as they were conceived of by the highest type of Greek. He thought to himself: I reverence the Divine in the little child, hence there is no need to concern myself with it in the first seven years of life. It can grow up in the family in which the Gods have placed it. Superearthly forces are still working in it from pre-earthly life. When the seventh year is reached it behoves humanity to become responsible for the development of the forces in the child. What must man do, then, when he knows how to pay true reverence to the Divine in the human being? What must he do as regards education? He must develop to the highest possible extent the human faculties that have unfolded in the child up to the seventh year. The divine power, the way in which the spiritual expresses itself in the body—this must be developed to the greatest possible extent. Thus the Gymnast had perforce to be convinced of the necessity for understanding the divine power in the human body and being able to develop it in the body. The same healing, life-sustaining forces which the child possesses from pre-earthly existence, and which have been fostered in a purely elementary way up to the change of teeth—these must be preserved from the seventh to the fourteenth year by human insight, by human art. Further education must then proceed wholly in accordance with the natural being. And so all education was 'gymnastic' because the divine education of the human being was seen as a 'gymnastic.' Man must continue the 'divine gymnastic' through his education.

This was more or less the attitude of the Greek to the child. He said to himself: If through my insight I am able to preserve in freshness and health the forces of growth which have developed in the child up to the seventh year; if I enable the forces which are there by nature up to the seventh year to remain through the whole of earthly life, right up to death, then I am educating in the best possible way. To see that the *'child' in the human being was not lost till death*—this was the great and mighty principle, the tremendously far-reaching maxim of Greek education. The Greek teacher thought: I must see to it that the human being can preserve for himself through the whole of his earthly life, right up to death, the forces of the child, that between the seventh and fourteenth years these forces retain their living nature. A tremendously far-reaching and deeply significant principle of education! And gymnastic exercises were based on the perception that the forces present up to the seventh year have in no way disappeared, but are merely slumbering within the human being and must be awakened from day to day. To waken the slumbering forces between the seventh and the fourteenth years, only to draw forth from the human being in this second period of life what was there by nature in the first period—this constituted Greek gymnastic education. The very greatness of his culture and civilization arose from the fact that the Greek—by introducing the right education—was at pains to preserve the 'child' in the human being right up to death. And when we wonder at this greatness we must ask ourselves: Can we imitate this ideal? We cannot, for it rests upon three postulates, without which it is unthinkable.

These three postulates must be remembered by the modern educationist when he looks back to Greece. The first thing to remember is the following:—These principles of education were only applied to a small portion of mankind, to a higher class, and they presuppose the existence of *slavery*. Without slavery it would not have been possible to educate a small class of mankind in this way. For in order to educate thus, part of man's work on the earth fell to the lot of those who were left to their elemental human destiny, without education in the true Greek sense. Greek civilization and Greek education are alike unthinkable without the existence of slavery. And so the delight of those who look back with inner satisfaction on what Greece accomplished in the evolutionary history of mankind, is tempered with the tragic realization that it was achieved at the cost of slavery.

The second postulate is the whole position of woman in Greek social life. The women lived a life withdrawn from the direct impulses at the root of Greek civilization, and it was this secluded life that alone made it possible for the child to be left, up to the seventh year, to the care of sheer instinct at home; for this instinct was cultivated without any knowledge whatever. Out of a human instinct the child was led on by the elemental forces of growth to the time of the change of teeth. It was necessary that the child's life up to this period should, despite its different nature, proceed just as unconsciously in the wider environment of the family, as the embryonic life had proceeded through the forces of nature. This was the second postulate.

The third is really something of a paradox to modern man, but he must, none the less, grow to understand it. The second point—the position of women in Greece—is easier to understand, for we know from a superficial observation of modern life that between the Greek age and our own time, as a result of what took place in the Middle Ages, women have sought to take their share in social life. And if we still wanted to be as Greek as the Greeks were, with the interest in conscious education confined exclusively to men, I wonder how small this audience would be if it were only made up of the men who were allowed to concern themselves with education!

The third postulate lies deeper down, and its nature makes it difficult for modern civilization to acknowledge. We attain our spiritual life by human effort, we have to attain it by active work. Anyone who observes the spiritual activities of civilized life will be obliged to admit that as regards the most important domain of civilized life, we must count upon what we shall achieve in the future by human activity. Observing all the human labour which has to be spent on the attainment of a spiritual life in present-day civilization, we look with some astonishment at the spiritual life of the ancient Greeks and especially of the ancient Orientals. For this spiritual life was simply there. A truth such as that of the part played in human life by the seventh year—a truth which modern man simply does not realize—was deeply rooted in Greece. (Outer symtoms indicate its significance, but modern culture is very far from understanding it.) It was one of the mighty truths that flowed through ancient spiritual life. And we stand in wonder before this spiritual life, when we learn to know what wisdom, what spiritual knowledge was once possessed by man.

If, without being confused by modern naturalistic and materialistic prejudices, we go back to early civilization, we find, at the beginning of historical life, a universal, penetrating wisdom according to which man directed his life. It was not an acquired wisdom, but it flowed to mankind through revelation, through a kind of inspiration. And it is this that modern civilization will not acknowledge. It will not recognize that a primal wisdom was bestowed spiritually upon man, and that he evolved it in such a way that, for instance, even in Greece, care was still taken to preserve the 'child' in man right up to earthly death. Now this revelation of primeval wisdom is no more to be found—a fact deeply connected with the whole evolution of man. Part of man's progress consists in the fact that the primal wisdom no longer comes to him without activity on his part, but that he must attain to wisdom through his own efforts. This is connected in an inner sense with the growth of the impulse of human freedom which is at present in its strongest phase. The progress of humanity does not ascend, as is so readily imagined, in a straight line from one stage to another. What man has to attain from out of his own being in the present age, he has to attain at the cost of losing that revelation from without, which held within itself the deepest of all wisdom.

The loss of primeval wisdom, the necessity to attain wisdom by man's own labours—this is related to the third postulate in Greek education. Greek education may fill us with admiration but it cannot be dissociated from these three factors: ancient slavery, the ancient position of woman, and the ancient relationship of spiritual wisdom to spiritual life. None of the three exists to-day, nor would they now be considered worthy of true human existence. We are living at a time when the following question arises: How ought we to educate, realizing as we do that these three *a priori* conditions have been swept away by human progress? And so we must observe the signs of the times, if we desire from inner depths to find the true impulse for our modern education.

. . . .

The whole of the so-called medieval development of man which followed the civilization of Greece and has indeed come right down to modern times, really proved by its very nature that in regard to education and methods of teaching, different paths must be struck from those of Greece, which were so well-fitted to an earlier age. The nature of man had, indeed, changed. The efficacy and reliability of Greek education were an outcome of the fact that it was based upon human 'habit'—upon that which can be built into the very structure of the human body.

Up to the change of teeth in the seventh year, the development of man's being is inwardly connected with the body.

The development of the body is such, however, that its functions are carried on as though unconsciously. Indeed it is only when the faculties work unconsciously that they are right; they are reliable only when what I have to do is implanted into the dexterity of my hands and is accomplished of itself, without need for further reflection. When practice has become habit—then I have achieved securely what I have to achieve through my body. The real aim of Greek life was to make the whole earthly existence of man a matter of 'habit' in this sense. From his education onwards till his death, all man's actions were to become habitual—so habitual that it should be impossible to leave them off. For when education is based on such a principle as this, the forces which are natural to the child up to the change of teeth, up to the seventh year, can be maintained; the child-forces can be maintained until earthly life ends with death.

Now what happened when, through historical circumstances, new peoples pouring over from the East to the West founded a new civilization during the Middle Ages, establishing themselves in Middle Europe and in the West—even in America? These peoples assimilated the qualities natural to the southern regions but their coming brought quite different habits of life to mankind. What was the result of this? It set up the conditions for a totally different kind of individual human development. In this time, for example, men came to the conscious realization that slavery ought not to be; to the realization that women must be respected. At this time it also became apparent that as regards the evolution of the individual, in the period between the seventh and fourteenth year—when development is no longer of a purely bodily nature but when the soul is to a certain degree emancipated from the body—the child in this period was not now susceptible of being treated as in earlier times. In effect, the conservation of the forces of early childhood in the boy between the ages of seven and fourteen that had been practised hitherto, was no longer possible.

This is the most significant historical phenomenon of the Middle Ages and of the times right up to our own, so far as this second period of life is concerned. And only to-day do we see the powerful forces which belong to the period when the fourteenth and fifteenth years have been passed and human nature rises up most strongly in revolt, when indeed it bears within itself the force of revolt.

How did this revolt in human nature express itself? The old primeval wisdom which flowed down naturally to the Greeks, came to be, in Roman and medieval tradition, something that was only preserved through books, through writing. Indeed it was only believed on the authority of tradition. The concept of faith—as it developed during the Middle Ages—did not exist in very ancient civilizations, nor even in the culture of the Greeks. It would have been so much nonsense in those times. The concept of belief only began to develop when the primeval wisdom no longer flowed directly into man, but was merely preserved. This still applies fundamentally to the greater part of humanity to-day. Everything of a spiritual, supersensible nature is tradition. It is 'believed', it is no longer immediate and actual. Nature and the perception of nature—this is an actuality, but all that refers to the supersensible, to supersensible life, is tradition. Up to the Middle Ages and beyond man gave himself up to this kind of tradition, thinking at times, it is true, that he did in fact experience these things. But the truth is that direct spiritual knowledge and revelation came to be preserved in written form, living from generation to generation as a heritage merely on the authority of tradition. This was the outer aspect. And what of the inner aspect? Let us now look back once again to Greece. In Greece faculties of soul developed as of themselves, as a result of the whole human being acquiring habits of life whereby the 'child' was preserved in man till death. Music proceeded from the breathing and blood circulation, intellect from gymnastic. Without being cultivated, a marvellous memory evolved in the Greeks as a result of the development of the habits of the body. We in our age have no longer any idea of the kind of memory that arose, even among the Greeks, without being cultivated in any way—and in the ancient East this was even more significant. The body was nurtured, habits were cultivated, and then the memory arose from the body itself. A marvellous memory was the outcome of a right culture of the body.

A living proof of the fact that we have no conception of the kind of memory possessed by the Greeks—a memory which in a wonderful way made it so easy for the spiritual treasures to be handed down and become a common good—is the fact that shorthand writers have to attend when lectures are given which people want to remember. This would have seemed absurd in Greek civilization; the memory truly preserved it all, being carried by the healthy proficiency of the body. The soul developed itself out of bodily proficiency. And having developed, the soul had before it the primal spiritual wisdom which came of itself as if through revelation. This primal spiritual wisdom disappeared, grew to be mere tradition. It had to be carried externally from generation to generation by the priesthood who preserved the traditions. And inwardly man was forced to begin to cultivate a faculty, whose cultivation the Greek had never thought of as a necessity. In education during the Middle Ages it became more and more necessary to cultivate the memory. Into the memory man inculcated what had been preserved by tradition.

Thus, historical tradition outwardly and remembrance and memory inwardly had to be cultivated by education. *Memory* was the first soul quality to be cultivated when the emancipation of the soul had taken place. And those who know what importance was attached to the memory in schools only a short while ago can form an opinion of how rigidly this cultivation of the memory has been preserved—as the result of an historical necessity.

And so through the whole of the Middle Ages education staggers on like a ship that cannot balance in a storm, for the soul of man is the most hard of access. To the body man can gain access; he can come to terms with the spirit, but the soul is so bound up with the individuality of man that it is the most inaccessible of all.

It was all a matter of the soul whether a man found the inner path to the authorities who preserved the tradition for him, whether his piety was great enough to enable him to receive the words in which the medieval priest-teacher inculcated the tradition into humanity; all this was an affair of the soul. And to cultivate the memory, without doing violence to another man's individuality, without subtly suggesting things one wants to suggest—this needs tact of soul. What was necessary for the soul-culture of the Middle Ages was as much heeded by tactful men as it was ignored by the tactless. Such was the condition of medieval education: a state of fluctuation between that which well became the human soul and that which wronged the human soul in its deepest being. And all unnoticed by men, much, very much from this medieval education has been preserved on into the present age.

Education during the Middle Ages assumed this character because, in the first place, the soul no longer wished to preserve the 'child'; for the soul itself was to be educated. And because of the conditions of the times the soul could only be educated through tradition and memory. Between the seventh and the fourteenth years the human being is, as it were, in a certain state of flux. The soul does not work in the same condition of security as is afforded by the bodily constitution up to the seventh year and the direction imparted by the spirit has not yet come into being. Everything is of a very intimate character—making piety and delicacy a necessity.

All these things affected education, with the result that, for a long period of human evolution it also entered into a vague and indefinite channel. This age during which tradition and memory had to be cultivated appears fraught with extraordinary difficulties for education. To-day we are living at a time when, as a result of the natural course of development, man desires another kind of certainty, different from that resting on such unstable ground in the Middle Ages. And this search for other foundations expresses itself in the innumerable efforts towards educational reform in our time. It is out of knowledge of this fact that Waldorf School education has arisen. Waldorf School education is based upon this question: How shall we educate in a time when the revolt in the soul between the seventh and fourteenth years of life against the conservation of 'childhood' is still going on? How shall we educate now that man, in addition to that, has in the modern age lost even the old medieval connection with tradition? Outwardly man has lost his faith in tradition. Inwardly he strives to be a free being—one who at every moment shall confront life unhampered. He does not wish to stand on a memory foundation all his life long. Such is modern man, who now desires to be inwardly free of tradition and of memory. And however much certain portions of our humanity to-day would like to preserve ancient customs—it simply will not do. The very existence of the many efforts for educational reform indicates that a great question is facing us. It was impossible in the Middle Ages to educate in the Greek way, and in our times education can no longer be based on tradition and memory. We have to educate in accordance with the immediate moment of life through which man is placed into his existence on earth—where he has to make his decisions as a free being out of the given facts of the moment. How, then, must we educate free human beings? That is the question which really for the first time to-day confronts humanity.

.   .   .   .

As the hour is getting late, I will bring these thoughts to a conclusion in a few words and postpone until to-morrow's lecture the consideration of the methods of education that are necessary at the present day.

In Greek education, the Gymnast must be recognized as one who preserved the forces of childhood on into the second period of life between the seventh and the fourteenth or fifteenth year. The 'child' must be preserved—so said the Greeks. The forces of childhood must remain in the human being to the time of earthly death—they must be conserved. The Greek educator, the Gymnast, has in general to foster what he could not but point to in the seven- to fourteen-year old child before him as its nature-foundation, its inherited nature-foundation. Out of his spiritual wisdom he had to know how to judge this and preserve it. Evolution in the Middle Ages went beyond this, and, as a result, our present age developed. Only now does the position of a modern man within the social order become a matter of consciousness. This fact of conscious life can only come into being after the age of puberty has been reached, after the fourteenth or fifteenth year. Then there appears in the human being something which I shall have repeatedly to describe in the following lectures as the consciousness of the real nature of inner freedom in the being of man. Then, indeed, man "comes to himself." And if, as it sometimes happens to-day, human beings believe themselves to have reached this consciousness before the fourteenth or fifteenth year, before the age of puberty, this is only an aping of later life. It is not a fundamental fact. It was this fundamental fact, which appears after the age of puberty, that the Greek purposely sought to avoid in the development of the individual man. The intensity with which he invoked nature, the 'child', into human existence, darkened and obscured full experience of this moment of consciousness after puberty. The human being passed through it in a dimmed consciousness, restrained by nature. The historical course of human evolution, however, is such that this is no longer possible. This conscious urge would burst forth with elemental, volcanic force after the age of puberty if attempts were made to hold it back.

During what we call the elementary school age, that is to say, between the seventh and fourteenth year, the Greek had to take into consideration the earliest nature-life of the child. We in our day have to take account of what follows puberty, of that which will be experienced after puberty in full human consciousness by the boy or girl whom we have been guiding for seven years. We may no longer suppress this into a dreamlike obscurity as did the Greeks, even the highest type of Greek, even Plato and Aristotle, who, in consequence, accepted slavery as a self-evident necessity. Because education was of such a kind that it obscured this all-important phenomenon of human life after puberty, the

Greek was able to preserve the forces of early childhood into the period of life between the seventh and fourteenth year.

We must be prophets of future humanity if we would educate in the right way. The Greek could rely upon instinct, for his task was to conserve the foundations laid by nature. We, as educator must be able to develop intuitions. We must anticipate all human qualities if we would become true educators, true teachers. For the essential thing in our education will be to give the child, between its seventh and fourteenth year, something that it can remember when the aforesaid consciousness sets in—a remembrance that looks with inner satisfaction at what we have implanted in its being, that lets it say "Yes" to us who have been its teacher. We educate in the wrong way to-day if, later on, when the child has gone out into life, it can no longer look back on us and say, "Yes!"

Thus there must arise teachers with intuition, teachers who enter once again upon the path along which the spiritual world and spiritual life can be attained by man, who can give the child between the seventh and fourteenth year all those things to which it can look back in later life with satisfaction. The Greek teacher was a preserver. He said: All that lived within the child in earlier life, slumbers within him after the seventh year, and this I must awaken. Of what nature must our education be to enable us to implant in the age of childhood that which later will awaken of itself in the free human being? We have to lead an education into the future. This makes it necessary that in our present epoch the whole situation of education must be different from what it was in the past. In Greece, education arose through devotion to what was of nature in the child. Education was a fact of nature which, as it were, played into human life, but as a result of how life as a whole has developed up to our time, it has worked itself out of its natural foundations.

As teachers in schools, this is what we must realize: We must offer to the child before us something to which it may be able to say "Yes!" when in later life it awakens to independent consciousness. The child must not only love us during school-days, but afterwards find this love for us justified by mature judgment. Otherwise education is only a half-education—therefore weak and ineffective. When we are conscious of this we shall realize to what a great extent education and instruction, from being a fact of nature that plays into the human being, must become a *moral* fact.

This is the deep inner struggle waged by those who from their innermost being have some understanding of the form which education must assume. They feel this, and it compresses itself into the question: How can we make education and instruction itself into a free act in the highest sense, that is, into a moral act in the highest degree ? How can education become out and out a moral concern of mankind ? This is the great problem before us to-day, and it must be solved, if the most praiseworthy efforts towards educational reform are to be rightly directed on into the future.

IV

THE CONNECTION OF THE SPIRIT WITH BODILY ORGANS

Education in any given epoch cannot but be according to the general form of civilization prevailing at the time. What the general form of civilization has to offer—that can be passed on to the child in its education by the teacher. When I was speaking of the Greeks, I told you that they possessed an intimate knowledge of the whole human being, and from this intimate knowledge were able to educate the child in a way that is no longer possible for us to-day. The knowledge of the whole human being possessed by the Greek was derived entirely from the human body. The body of man was in a certain sense transparent to him. The body unveiled, revealed to him both soul and spirit, as far as his understanding of these allowed. We have seen how the Greeks educated the whole human being by taking the body as the starting-point. All that could not be drawn out of the body, in the sense in which I showed that music was drawn out of it, was imparted to the human being comparatively late in life, indeed only after his bodily education had been completed, at about the twentieth year or even later.

We to-day are in quite a different position. The very greatest illusions in human evolution are really due to the belief that ancient epochs—where we have to do with a totally different humanity—can be revived. But in this present age particularly it behoves us to turn entirely and with practical common sense to reality. And if we understand this historical reality, we can only say: Just as the Greeks had to direct the whole of their education from out of the body, so have we to direct ours from out of the spirit. We have to find ways of approaching even bodily education from out of the spirit. For whether we like it or no, mankind has now come to a point where it must grasp the spirit as such, it must win the spirit for itself, as its own human content, through human work.

Now it is just when we desire to educate in accordance with the needs of our epoch, that we feel how little progress has been made by civilization in general, in respect of this permeation by the spirit. And then there arises the longing to make the spirit more and more man's own possession.

Where do we find, let us say at a comparatively high level, the conception of the spirit possessed by modern humanity? You must not be shocked if I characterize this by examples from the height of modern spiritual life. That which appears at the top merely symbolically, and within the limits of the cultural life, rules, in reality, the whole of civilization. In the course of our endeavour to grasp what spirit is, we have only to-day reached the stage of apprehending the spirit in ideas, in thinking. And perhaps the best way to understand human thinking in our age, in its greatest scope, is to observe this modern thought as it appears, let us say, in John Stuart Mill or in Herbert Spencer. I asked you not to be shocked by the fact that I point to the highest level of culture. For that which in John Stuart Mill and Herbert Spencer appears merely, so to say, as an outstanding symptom, in reality dominates every sphere and is the characteristic thinking of our civilization. When, therefore, we ask to-day: How do men know the spirit, out of which they are to educate just as the Greek educated the body? We have to answer that men know the spirit just as John Stuart Mill or Herbert Spencer knew it. Now how did they know it? Let us think for a moment of the idea people have to-day when they speak of the spirit. I do not here mean that nebulous and absolutely indefinite image hovering somewhere "above the clouds", which is meant where the spirit is spoken of to-day. This is something that tradition has imparted and there is no actual experience connected with it. We can only speak of the spirit possessed by humanity when we observe how humanity deals with this spirit, how it works and what it does with it.

And the spirit in our present civilization is the spirit which John Stuart Mill and Herbert Spencer have already worked into their philosophies. There indeed it is and there it has to be sought. What we must observe is the way in which men apply the spirit, not the way in which they speak about it abstractly.

And now let us consider this "thought out" spirit, for in our time the spirit is mainly no more than something thought, a spirit capable perhaps, of thinking philosophically. Compared with the full content perceived by the Greek however when he spoke of man, of *Anthropos*, the element in which we flit about in spirit when we think, is something—well—distilled, attenuated to the highest degree. When he spoke of man, the Greek had always the picture of bodily man before him and the bodily man was at once a revelation of soul and spirit. This man was somewhere, at some time; this man had limits; he was bounded by his skin. And those who trained this man in the Greek gymnasium covered his skin with oil in order to emphasize this boundary. Man was a wholly concrete entity, existing somewhere at some time, and formed in one way or another.

And now think of the thinking in which we lay hold of the spirit to-day. Where is it ? What form has it got ? It is all indefinite, there is never a "how" or "when"; never any definite form, never any imagery. People do try indeed to build up some kind of image, but let us look at John Stuart Mill's idea of imagery, for instance. He said: When a man thinks, one idea is followed by a second and a third. Man thinks indeed in ideas—which are the inward images of words. He thinks in ideas and the ideas get associated with one another. This really is the essence of the discovery: one idea links on to a second, third, fourth, and so on. The ideas associate themselves. And modern psychology speaks in the most varied ways of associations of ideas as the real inner essence of spiritual life. Now suppose we were to ask: What kind of feeling and perception of our own being as man should we have if this association of ideas were indeed what we obtained as spirit ? We stand in the world; now the ideas begin to move; they associate themselves. And now we look back upon ourselves, upon what we really are, as spirit, in these associated ideas. This leads to a consciousness of the self that is exactly like the consciousness a man would have if he were to look at himself in a mirror and see a skeleton!—and moreover a dead skeleton. Think of the shock you would have if you were to look in the mirror and see a skeleton! In the skeleton it is so that the bones are associated with each other, they are held together by external means and are fixed one above the other, according to mechanical law. In our idea of the spirit, therefore, we merely copy mechanics. To those who have a full sense of manhood, who feel healthy, and are in a human sense healthy, it is actually as though they were to look at themselves in a mirror and see their spirit composed of bones—for in the books describing association-psychology one sees oneself as in a mirror. We may have this pleasure constantly (not, of course, in the external, bodily sense), for it arises whenever we compare the modern state of affairs with the Greek. Spiritually, we have this experience again and again. We go to our philosophers, thinking that they may be able to give us self-knowledge, and they place their books before us as a mirror in which we see ourselves as a bony spectre in associations of ideas.

This is what takes hold of a man to-day when he tries to think in a practical way about education and to approach it from the standpoint of our general civilization. No indication of what education ought to be is given him, but he is shown how to find a heap of bones and how to piece together a skeleton. This is how the ordinary man feels to-day. He longs for a new education, and everywhere the question arises: How ought we to educate? But where can he turn? He can only turn to the general form of civilization, and this civilization shows him that all he can build up is a skeleton. And now what I might call a strong feeling for civilization must take possession of the human being. If his feeling is healthy, he must be able to feel himself permeated by this intellectualistic nature of modern thought and ideas. And it is in regard to this that the modern man is confused. He would like to think that what the mirror reveals is sublime and perfect; he would like to be able to make something of it, above all, he would like to make use of it in education—but he cannot. One cannot educate with this.

If we are to have the necessary enthusiasm as educators, therefore, we must learn in the first place to perceive all that is not living, but dead, in our intellectualistic culture—for the skeleton is a dead thing. And if we saturate ourselves with the knowledge that our thinking is dead, we very soon discover that all death proceeds from the living. If you were to find a corpse, you would not take it as the original thing. You would only think of a corpse as something in itself if you had no conception of a human being. If, however, you have a conception of what a human being is, you know that the corpse is something that has been left behind. From the nature of the corpse, you conclude that the human being was once there. If you recognize the kind of thinking that is cultivated to-day as being a thing dead, as being a corpse, you can relate it to something living. Moreover you then have the inner impulse to make this thinking living and so to revitalize the whole of our civilization. It will then be possible for something practical to emerge from our modern civilization, something that can reach the living man, not merely the skeleton-man, just as the Greeks reached the living man in their education.

Let us not undervalue the importance of the feelings with which a teacher can set out and, indeed, must set out. The teachers at the Wardorf School were first of all given a Seminary Course. It was not merely a question of following the points of a given programme, but of imparting a quite definite condition of soul, leading back what our age takes such pride in as its heritage into relation with the innermost being of man, in order to make dead thinking into living thinking, neutral thinking into thinking full of character, natural inorganic thinking into thinking penetrated by the whole man, indeed into truly human thinking. In the first place, then, thoughts must begin really to live in the teacher.

Now when a thing lives, something follows from this life.

The human being who has definite place in space and time, who has spirit, soul, body, a definite form and boundary, does not merely think; he also feels and wills. And when a thought is communicated to him, this thought is the germ both of a feeling and an impulse of will; it becomes a complete thing. The ideal of our modern thinking is to be what people call " objective," as motionless as possible—in short to be a motionless reflection of the outer world and a mere handmaiden of experience. It contains no force; no impulse of feeling and of will arise from it.

The Greek took his start from the bodily man who was there before him. We must take our start—and everyone feels this to be true—from a human ideal, but this ideal must not be merely theoretical; it must live and it must contain the force of feeling and will. The first thing needful when we think about a change in education to-day is that we grow beyond abstract and theoretical ideals. For when we receive these into our souls they cannot become feeling and will within us, they cannot bring humanity into us, down into our physical body.

Our thoughts do not become gestures, and they must become so once more. They must not only be received by the child who sits passively, but they must move arms and hands and guide him when he passes out into the world. Then we shall have unified human beings—for we must again educate unified human beings; we shall have human beings whose bodily education is a continuance of what we have given them in the schoolroom. People do not think like this nowadays. They think that what is given in the schoolroom is so much intellectualism, something that it is necessary to give. But it fatigues and strains the human being, perhaps even causes nervous troubles. Something else must be added—so it is felt—and then bodily exercises are added as an " extra." And so to-day we have two quite separate branches: intellectual education and bodily training. The one does not promote the other. We have really two human beings, one nebulous and hypothetical and one real, and we do not understand this real man as the Greek understood him. We squint, as it were, when we observe a human being, for there seem to be two in front of us. We must again learn to " see straight," to see the whole being of man as a unity, a totality. This is to begin with, the most important thing of all in education.

. . . .

What we must do, therefore, is to press forward beyond the more or less theoretical maxims of education in existence to-day to an education that is practical in the real sense of the word. From what I have said, it follows that much depends upon how we again bring the spirit, which we really only grasp intellectually, to the human being, so that this vague, nebulous spirit with which we observe men, shall become *Man*. We must learn how to behold man in the spirit, as the Greeks beheld him in the body.

As a preliminary to-day, let me give an example which will explain how, from out of the spirit, we can begin to understand the human being right down into the body. As an example, I will choose the way in which the spirit may be connected with a definite organ in the human being. I choose the most striking example, but merely provisionally. These things will become more definite in the following lectures. Let me show you a process which the Greeks too, considered to be deeply symbolical and of extraordinary significance in the development of the child: the coming of the teeth. The time of the change of the teeth was, in Greece, the age at which the child was given over to public education. And now let us try to envisage the relation of the spirit to the human teeth. It will seem strange that in discussing man as a spiritual being, I speak first of the teeth. It only seems strange because, as the result of their modern culture, people are quite familiar with the form of a tiny animal germ when they look through the microscope, but they know very little about what lies before them. It is realized that the teeth are necessary for eating—that to begin with is the most striking thing about them. It is also known that they are necessary for speech, that sounds are connected with them, that the air flows in a particular way from the lungs and the larynx, through the lips and palate, and that certain consonants have to be formed by the teeth. It is known, therefore, that the teeth serve a useful purpose in eating and speaking.

Now a truly spiritual understanding of the human being shows us something else as well. If you are able to study man in the way I described in the first lecture, it will dawn on you that the child develops teeth not only for the sake of eating and speaking, but for quite a different purpose as well. Strange as it sounds to-day, the child develops teeth for the purpose of thinking. Modern science little knows that the teeth are the most important of all organs of thought. In the little child before the change of teeth, the physical teeth as such are the most important organ of thought. As the child in its interplay with the environment finds its way spontaneously into thinking, as the life of thought rises up from the dim sleeping and dreaming life of infancy, the whole process is connected with the teeth pressing through in the head, it is bound up with the forces that are pressing outwards from the head. The forces that press the teeth out from the jaw are the same forces that now within the soul bring thought to the surface from the undefined sleeping and dreaming life of childhood. With the same degree of intensity as it teethes, the child learns to think.

Now how does the child learn to think? It learns to think because it is an imitative being and as such is wholly given up to its environment. Right into its innermost being it imitates what is going on in its environment and what happens in this environment under the impulses of thoughts. In exactly the same measure as thought then springs up in the child—in exactly the same measure do the teeth emerge. In effect, the force that appears in the soul as thinking lies within these teeth.

Let us now follow the further development of the child. About the seventh year, the child undergoes the change of teeth. He gets his second teeth. I have already said that the force which produces the first and second teeth has been present in the whole organism of the child—only it shows itself in the strongest form in the head. The second teeth only come once. The forces which drive the second teeth out from the organism of the child do not work again as physical forces in the course of earthly life. They become powers of the soul, powers of the spirit; they vivify the inner being of the human soul. Thus, when we observe the child about the seventh and fourteenth year of life, with particular regard to his characteristic qualities of soul, we find that what now appears between the seventh and fourteenth years as qualities of soul, especially in the child's thinking, was a force of the organs up to the seventh year. It worked in the physical organism, forced out the teeth, reached its culmination as physical force with the change of teeth, and then changed itself into an activity of soul.

These things can, of course, only be truly observed when one presses forward to the mode of cognition, which I described in a previous lecture as the first stage of exact clairvoyance, as Imaginative knowledge. The abstract, intellectual knowledge of the human being that is common to-day does not lead to this other kind of knowledge. Thought must vivify itself from within so that it becomes imaginative, so that through thought as such one can really grasp something. Nothing whatever can really be grasped by intellectualistic thinking; with it the objects all remain external. One looks at them and forms mental images of what one sees. But thinking can be inwardly re-inforced, it can be made active. Then one no longer has abstract intellectualistic thoughts but imaginative pictures, which now fill the soul in place of the intellectual thoughts. At the first stage of exact clairvoyance —as I have described it—one can perceive indeed how, besides the forces of the physical body, there is working in man a supersensible body, if you will forgive the paradoxical expression. This is the first supersensible member of the human being. Now what are the characteristics of the physical body of man? It can be weighed; it strives in the direction of gravity, is subject to the force of gravity. Its outstanding characteristic is that it can be weighed. If through Imaginative knowledge we become aware of the supersensible body of man which I have called in my books the etheric body, or body of formative forces, we find that it cannot be weighed. It weighs nothing; on the contrary, it strives away from the earth towards every part of cosmic space. It contains the forces that are opposed to gravity, and strives perpetually against gravity.

Just as ordinary physical knowledge teaches us of the physical body of man, so does Imaginative knowledge, the first stage of exact clairvoyance, teach us of the etheric body that is always striving to get away from earthly gravity. And just as we gradually learn to relate the physical body to its environment, so do we learn to relate the etheric body to its environment.

In studying the physical body of man, we look outside in nature, in material nature, for the substances of which it is composed. We realize that everything in man which is subject to gravity, his heaviness, his weight—all this has weight in outer nature as well. It enters into man through the assimilation of nourishment. In this way we obtain, as it were, a natural conception of the human organism in so far as the organism is physical. Similarly, through Imaginative knowledge we obtain a conception of the relationship of the self-enclosed etheric body or body of formative forces in man to the surrounding world. That which, in spring, drives the plants out of the soil, against gravity, in all directions towards the cosmos, that which organizes the plants, brings them into relation with the upward-working stream of light, that which as the chemistry of the plant is at work as it strives upwards—all this must be related to the etheric body of man, just as salt, cabbage, turnip and meat are related to the physical body. Thus in the first stage of exact clairvoyance, this thinking which is a unity and self-sufficient, is concerned with the etheric body or body of formative forces of man —this " second man," as it were. Up to the change of teeth, this etheric body of formative forces is most intimately bound up with the physical body. There, from within, it organizes the physical body; it is the force which drives out the teeth. When the human being gets his second teeth, the part of the etheric body that drives the teeth out has no more to do for the physical body. Its activity is emancipated, as it were, from the physical body. With the change of teeth the inner etheric forces which have pressed the teeth out are freed, and with these etheric forces we carry on the free thought that begins to assert itself in the child from the seventh year onwards. The force of the teeth is no longer a physical force as it was in the child during the time when the teeth are the organs of thought; it is now an etheric force. But it is the same force which produced the teeth and is now working in the etheric body which now thinks. When we feel ourselves as thinking human beings, and feel that thinking proceeds from the head—many people only have this experience when thinking has brought on a headache—a true knowledge shows us that the force with which we think from out of the head is the same as the force which was once contained in the teeth.

Thus our knowledge brings us near to the unity of the being of man. We learn once again how the physical is connected with what is more of the soul. We know that the child first thinks with the forces of the teeth, and this is why teething troubles are so inwardly bound up with the whole life of the child. Think of all that happens when the child is teething! All these teething troubles arise because the process of teething through its connection with thinking is so intimately connected with the innermost life, with the innermost spirituality of the child. The growth-forces of the teeth are freed and become the forces of thought in the human being, the free, independent force of thought. If we have the necessary gift of observation, we can see this process of becoming independent; we see how quite exactly with the change of teeth, thinking emancipates itself from bondage to the body. And what happens now? In the first place the teeth become the helpers of what permeates thoughts, they become helpers of speech. The teeth, which had, at first, the independent task of growing in accordance with the forces of thought, are now pressed down one stage, as it were. Thinking, which now no longer takes place in the physical body but in the etheric body, descends one stage. This already happens during the first seven years, for the whole process goes on successively, merely reaching its culmination with the coming of the second teeth. But then, when thought seeks expression in speech, the teeth become the helpers of thought.

And so, we look at the human being; we see his head. In the head the growth-forces of the teeth free themselves and become the force of thinking. Then, pressed down, as it were, into speech, we have all the processes for which the teeth are no longer directly responsible, because the etheric body now takes over the responsibility. The teeth become the helpers of speech. In this, their relationship with thought is still apparent. When we understand how the dental sounds find their way into the whole process of thinking, how man takes the teeth to his aid when through sounds like *d* or *t*, he brings the definite thought-element into speech, we again see in the dental sounds the particular task performed by the teeth.

I have shown you by this example of the teeth—which may perhaps seem very grotesque—how we come to understand the human being from out of the spirit. If we proceed in this way, thinking gradually ceases to be an abstract drifting in associated ideas, but connects itself with man, it reaches man. Then we no longer see merely physical functions in the human being, such as biting with the teeth or, at most, one's movements in the dental sounds of speech, but the teeth become for us an outer picture, an imagination in nature, of the process of thinking. Thinking, as it were, flashes forth and reveals itself by way of the teeth: Look, it says, there in the teeth is my outer countenance! When we really come to understand the teeth, thought that is otherwise abstract and nebulous assumes definite picture-form. We see how thought is working in the head at the place where the teeth lie, and how thought develops from the first to the second teeth. The whole process again takes on formative boundaries. A real image of the spirit begins to arise in nature herself. The spirit is once again creative.

We do not need only an anthropology which studies the human being in a wholly external way, and associates the elements of his being just as the different properties of ideas are associated. What we need is a kind of thinking that is not afraid to press onwards to the inner being of man, nor to speak of how the spirit becomes teeth and works in the teeth. This indeed is what we need, for then we penetrate into the being of man from the spirit. And then the something artistic arises. The abstract, theoretical and unpractical mode of observation, which merely evolves a human being with a skeleton-like thinking must be led over into the pictorial. Theoretical observation passes over into artistic perception, artistic creation. One has to form a picture of the teeth, at the same time as one strives to perceive the spirit working within them. The artistic, then, begins to be the guide to the first stage of exact clairvoyance—that of Imaginative knowledge. Here we begin to understand man in his real being. Man otherwise is only an abstraction in our thinking to-day.

Now in education, the being with whom we find ourselves confronted is the real man. He stands there, but there is an abyss between us, for we stand here with our abstract spirit. We must cross this abyss. We must, before all else, show how we can cross it. All we know of man to-day is how to put a cap on his head! We do not know how to put the spirit into his whole being, and this we must learn to do. We must learn how to clothe the human being inwardly, spiritually, just as we have learned how to clothe him externally, so that the spirit is treated just as the outer vesture is treated. When we approach the human being in this way, we shall attain to a living pedagogy and a living didactic.

. . . .

Just as the period of life at about the seventh year is significant in earthly existence on account of all the facts which I have described, so, similarly, is there a point in the earthly life of man which, on account of the symptoms which then arise in life, is no less significant. The actual points of time indicated are, of course, approximate, occurring in the case of some human beings earlier, in others later. The indication of seven-yearly periods is approximate. But round about the fourteenth or fifteenth year there is once more a time of extraordinary importance in earthly existence. This is the period when puberty is reached. But puberty, the emergence of the life of sex, is only the most external symptom of a complete transformation that has taken place in the being of man between the seventh and fourteenth year. Just as we must seek in the growth-forces of the teeth—in the human head—for the physical origin of thought that frees itself about the seventh year of life, and becomes a function of soul, so we must look for the activity of the second soul-force, namely feeling, in other parts of the human organism.

Feeling releases itself much later than thinking from the bodily nature, from the physical constitution of the human being. And between the seventh and fourteenth year the child's feeling-life is still inwardly bound up with its physical organization. Thinking is already free; feeling is still inwardly bound up with the body. All the feelings of joy, of sorrow and of pain that express themselves in the child still have a strong physical correlation with the secretions of the organs, the acceleration or retardation, speed or slackening of the breathing system. If our perception is keen enough, we can observe in these very phenomena the great transformation that is taking place in the life of feeling, when the outer symptoms of the change make their appearance. Just as the appearance of the second teeth denotes a certain climax of growth, so the close of the subsequent life-period—when feeling is gradually released from its connection with the body and becomes a soul function—is expressed in speech. This may be observed most clearly in boys. The voice changes; the larynx reveals the change. Just as the head reveals the change which lifts thinking out of the physical organism, the breathing system—the seat of the organic rhythmic activity—expresses the emancipation of feeling. Feeling detaches itself from the bodily constitution and becomes an independent function of soul. We know how this expresses itself in the boy. The larynx changes and the voice gets deeper. In the girl different phenomena appear in bodily growth and development, but this is only the external aspect.

Anyone who has reached the first stage of exact clairvoyance already referred to, the stage of imaginative perception, knows—for he perceives it—that the male physical body transforms the larynx at about the fourteenth year of life. The same thing happens in the female sex to the etheric body, or body of formative forces. The change withdraws to the etheric body, and the etheric body of the female takes on—as etheric body—a form exactly resembling the physical body of the male. Again, the etheric body of the male at the fourteenth year takes on a form resembling the physical body of the female. However extraordinary it may appear to a mode of knowledge that clings to the physical, it is nevertheless the case that from this all important period of life onwards, the man bears within him etherically the woman, and the woman etherically the man. This is expressed differently in the corresponding symptoms in the male and female.

Now if one reaches the second stage of exact clairvoyance —it is described in greater detail in my books—if, beyond Imagination, one attains to Inspiration—the actual perception of the independently spiritual that is no longer bound up with the physical body of man—then one becomes aware how, in actual fact, in this important period round about the fourteenth and fifteenth years, a third human member develops into a state of independence. In my books I have called this third being the astral body, according to an older tradition. (You must not be jarred by expressions, words have to be employed for everything.) This astral body is more essentially of the nature of soul than the etheric body; indeed the astral body is already of the soul and spirit. It is the third member of man and constitutes the second supersensible member of his being.

Up to the fourteenth or fifteenth year this astral body works through the physical organism and, at the fourteenth or fifteenth year, becomes independent. Thus there devolves upon the teacher a most significant task, namely to help the development to independence of this being of soul and spirit which lies hidden in the depths of the organism up to the seventh or eighth year and then gradually—for the process is successive—frees itself. It is this gradual process of detachment that we must assist, if we have the child to teach between the ages of seven and fourteen. And then, if we have acquired the kind of knowledge of which I have spoken, we notice how the child's speech becomes quite a different thing. The crude science of to-day—if I may call it so—concerns itself merely with the crude soul-qualities of the human being, and speaks of the other phenomena as secondary sexual characteristics. To spiritual observation, however, the secondary phenomena are primary, and vice versa.

These metamorphoses, the whole way in which feeling withdraws itself from the organs of speech, are of extraordinary significance. And as teachers and educators it is our wonderful task—a task that really inspires one's innermost being—gradually to release speech from the bodily constitution. How wonderful in a child of seven are the natural, spontaneous movements of the lips which come from organic activity! When the seven-year-old child utters the labial sounds, it is quite different from the way in which the child of fourteen or fifteen utters them. When the seven-year-old child utters the labial sounds it is an organic activity; it is the circulation of the blood, of the fluids, which involuntarily shoots into the lips. When the child reaches his twelfth, thirteenth or fourteenth years, this organic activity is transferred into the organism proper and the soul activity of feeling has to emerge and to move the lips voluntarily, which bring the element of feeling in speech to expression.

Just as the thought-element in speech, the hard thought-element, is manifested in the teeth, so is the soft, loving element of feeling manifested in the lips. And it is the labial sounds which impart warmth and loving sympathy to speech—sympathy with another being and the conveying of it. This marvellous transition from an organic activity of the lips to an activity brought into play by the soul, this development of the lips in the organic-psychological nature of the human being is a thing which the teacher can accompany, and thereby a most wonderful atmosphere can be brought into the school. For just as we see the supersensible, etheric element that permeates the body emerging at the seventh year of life as independent thinking-power, so do we see the element of independent soul and spirit emerging at the age of fourteen or fifteen. As teachers we help to bring the soul and spirit to birth. What Socrates meant is seen at a higher level.

In the following lectures I shall explain the new elements that appear in walking, in movement, when the human being is twenty or twenty-one years old—in the third period of life. It is enough to-day to have shown how thinking emancipates itself from organic activity and how feeling goes on emancipating itself from organic activity until the fourteenth or fifteenth year; to have shown how this gives us insight into man's development and how an otherwise merely abstract mode of thinking becomes a picture, an " imagination "; to have shown also how that which finds expression in human speech, in words, actually appears in its true form as soul and spirit when the human being reaches his fourteenth or fifteenth year.

Hence it can be said that if we would reach the human being from out of thought in a living way, if we would bring the spirit in its livingness to man, we must enter into the artistic. If we would bring feeling, the spiritual in feeling, the feeling spirit to man, we must not merely set about this with an artistic mood as in the former case, but also with a religious mood. For the religious mood alone can penetrate to the reality of the spirit.

Education between the seventh and fourteenth year, therefore, can only be carried on in the truly human sense when it is carried on in an atmosphere of religion, when it becomes almost a sacramental office—not, of course, in a sentimental, but in a truly human sense. And so we see how what man does comes streaming in when he brings life and soul to his otherwise abstract thinking, thinking that merely arises from the association of ideas. We see how he finds the way to an artistic apprehension of man, to an apprehension of man within the religious life. Art and religion are thus united with education. And so the way becomes clear from the question of the pupil to that of the teacher when we realize that pedagogy should become so practical, so clear and so living a knowledge that the teacher can only be a true educator of youth when he is able inwardly to become a thoroughly artistic, a thoroughly religious man.

V

THE EMANCIPATION OF THE WILL IN THE HUMAN ORGANISM

In yesterday's lecture I tried to show how thinking and feeling become independent at about the seventh and fourteenth year of life respectively, and release themselves from the bodily constitution of the human being. To-day I want to show how the will in the being of man gradually presses on to its independence during the process of growth.

The human will really remains bound up with the organism longest of all. Until about the twentieth or twenty-first year of life, the whole human will is intensively dependent on organic activity. It is dependent on the organic activity which develops particularly through the way in which the breathing is continued into the blood-circulation, and in which, through the inner fire, the inner warmth which has been developed, the blood-circulation in its turn takes hold of the motor organisation. It lays hold of the force arising in legs, feet, arms and hands when man moves and transforms it into a manifestation of the will.

It may be said that everything of the nature of will in the child, even including " children " between the ages of fifteen and twenty-one, is dependent upon the manner in which the forces of the organism play over into movement. The teacher above all men must cherish the power for unprejudiced observation of such things. He must be able to notice that a child is energetic, or has the predisposition to be energetic in his will if, when he walks, he places the back of his foot, his heel, firmly on the ground and that he is endowed with a less energetic will if he uses the front part of his foot and has a tripping gait.

All this, however, the way in which the legs are placed, the capacity to prolong the movement of the arms into dexterity of the fingers—all this is still an outer, physical manifestation of the will in the boy or girl, even after the fifteenth year. Only at about the twentieth year does the will release itself from the organism in the same way as feeling releases itself about the fourteenth year and thinking about the seventh year at the change of teeth. The external processes that are revealed by the freed thinking, however, are very striking and can readily be perceived; the change of teeth is a remarkable phenomenon in human life. The emancipation of feeling is less so; it expresses itself in the development of the so-called secondary sexual organs—their growth in the boy, the corresponding transformation in the girl—the change of voice in the boy and the change of the inner life-habits of the girl, and so forth. Here, the external symptoms of the metamorphosis in the human being are less striking. Feeling, therefore, becomes independent of the physical constitution in a more inward sense.

The outer symptoms of the emancipation of the will at about the twentieth or twenty-first year are still less apparent and are therefore practically unnoticed by an age like ours, which lives in externalities. In our time—in their own opinion—human beings are " grown-up " when they have reached the age of fourteen or fifteen. Our young people will not recognize that between the fifteenth and twenty-first year they should be acquiring not only outer knowledge but developing inner character and, above all, the will. Even before the age of twenty-one they set up as reformers, as teachers, and instead of applying themselves to what they can learn from their elders, they begin to write pamphlets and things of that kind. This is quite understandable in an age that is directed to the externalities of life. The decisive change that takes place about the twentieth or twenty-first year is hidden from such an age because it is wholly of an inner kind. But there is such a change and it may be described in the following way.

Up to his twenty-first year of life—approximately of course—man is not a self-contained personality; he is strongly subject to earthly gravity, to the earth's force of attraction. He struggles with earthly gravity until about the twenty-first year. And in this connection, external science will make many discoveries that are already known to the " exact clairvoyance " of which I spoke yesterday.

In our blood, in the blood corpuscles, we have iron. Until about the twenty-first year, the nature of these blood corpuscles is such that their gravity preponderates. From the twenty-first year onwards, the being of man receives an upward impulse from below; an upward impulse is given to all his blood. From the twenty-first year he sets the sole of his foot on the earth otherwise than he did before. This, indeed, is not known to-day but it is a fact of fundamental importance for the understanding of the human being so far as education is concerned. From the twenty-first year onwards, with every tread of the foot there works through the human organism from below upwards a force which did not work before. Man becomes a being complete in himself, one who has paralysed the downward-working forces by forces which work from below upwards, whereas before this age all the force of his growth and development flowed downwards from the head. This downward stream of forces is strongest of all in the little child up to the seventh year of life. The whole process of bodily organization during this period has its start in the head-organism. Up to the seventh year the head does everything and only when thinking is set free with the change of teeth, does the head also release itself from this strong downward-streaming force.

A great deal is known to-day about positive and negative magnetism; a great deal is known about positive and negative electricity—but very little indeed is known about what is going on in man himself. The fact that the forces streaming from the head to the feet and from the feet to the head are only organized in the course of the first two decades of life, is an anthroposophical truth of great significance—fundamentally significant, indeed, for the whole of education. It is a truth of which people to-day are wholly unconscious. And yet all education is really based on this question. For why do we educate ? That is the great question.

Standing as we do within the human and not in the animal kingdom, we have to ask ourselves: Why do we educate? Why is it that the animals grow up and carry out the functions of their lives without education? Why is it really necessary for us to educate human beings? Why is it that the human being cannot acquire what he needs in life merely through observation and imitation? Why has a teacher to intervene in the child's freedom? This is a question that is practically never raised, because these things are taken as a matter of course. But one can only become a true teacher when one ceases to take this question as a matter of course, when one realizes that it is an interference with the child to stand in front of him and want to educate him. Why should the child put up with it? We regard it as our obvious business to educate our children—but in their subconscious life they do not. And so we talk a great deal about the children's naughtiness and it never occurs to us that in their subconscious life—not in clear consciousness—we must appear very comic to the children when we teach them something from outside. They are quite justified in their immediate feeling of antipathy. And the great question for education is this: How can we change what at the outset is bound to be unsympathetic to children into something sympathetic? Now it is the opportunity to do this that is given between the seventh and fourteenth year. For at the seventh year, the head—which is the bearer of thinking—becomes independent. It no longer generates the downward-flowing forces so strongly as it did in the child up to the seventh year. It settles down, as it were, and looks after its own affairs.

Now only when we make the leap over into the fourteenth or fifteenth year do the organs of movement assume a personal nature of will. The will now becomes independent in the organs of movement. The forces flowing from below upwards, which man must have as forces of will, begin to work for the first time. For all will works from below upwards; all thought from above downwards. The direction of thought is from heaven to earth; the direction of will from earth to heaven. These two functions are not bound up with each other, not inserted into each other, between the seventh and fourteenth year. In the middle system of man, where breathing and circulation live and whence they originate, there lives also the feeling-nature of man which frees itself during this period. And if we rightly develop the feeling-nature between the seventh and fourteenth year, we set up a true relationship between the downward-flowing and the upward-flowing forces. It comes to no less than this, that between the child's seventh and fourteenth year, we have to bring his thinking into a right relationship with his will, with his willing. And in this it is possible to fail. It is on this account that we have to educate the human being, for in the animal this interplay of thinking and willing—in so far as the animal has dreamlike thought and has will—comes about of itself. In the human being, the interplay of thought and will does not come about of itself. In the animal, the process is natural; in the human being it must become a moral process. And because here on earth man has the opportunity of bringing about this union of his thinking with his willing, therefore it is that he can become a moral being. The whole character of man—in so far as it proceeds from the inner being—depends upon the true harmony being established, between thinking and willing, by human activity. The Greeks brought about this harmonization of thinking and willing by again to some extent calling into play, in their gymnastics, the stream of forces flowing from the head into the limbs—which is there naturally in the earliest years of life—and allowing the arms and legs so to move in dancing and wrestling that the head-activity was inserted into the limbs. Now we cannot return to Greek culture nor have that civilization over again. We must take our start from the spirit. And so we must understand how, in the twenty-first year, the will of man is freed as a result of the inner processes in the organs of movement which have been described, just as feeling was freed at the fourteenth year and thinking at the seventh year.

Modern civilization is mostly not awake to this. It has slept away its insight into the fact that education must consist in bringing the will—which appears in full freedom as a quality of soul about the twentieth year—into union with the thinking that is already released at the seventh year. We only acquire true reverence for the development of the human being when we bring the spirit into contact with the bodily nature of man, as we showed yesterday with regard to thinking and feeling and as we have just tried to show with regard to the will. We must see the will at work in the organs of movement, in the quite distinctive movement of fingers and arms, in the personal tread of the feet when the twentieth or twenty-first year is reached. Preparation for this has, however, been going on since the fifteenth year. If we can thus get back a spirit that is no more a mere association of ideas, a skeleton spirit, but a living spirit which can now even perceive how a man walks, how he moves his fingers, then we have again come back to man, then we can again educate.

The Greeks still had this power of perception instinctively. It was gradually lost, but only very slowly. It continued as a tradition down to the sixteenth century, and the most conspicuous thing about the sixteenth century is that civilized humanity as a whole loses an understanding of the relation between thinking and willing. Since the sixteenth century people have begun to reflect about education, and yet have no regard for the weightiest problems in the understanding of man. They do not understand man and they want to educate him. This is the tragedy that has existed since the sixteenth century and has continued on into our present age.

People feel and realize nowadays that a metamorphosis must begin in education. On all sides educational unions and leagues for educational reform are springing up. People feel that education needs something, but they do not approach the fundamental problem, which is this: How can one harmonize thinking and willing in the human being? At most they say: " There is too much intellectualism; we must educate less intellectually, we must educate the will." Now the will must not be educated for its own sake. All talk as to which is best, the education of thought or the education of will, is amateurish. This question alone is really practical and pertinent to the nature of man: How can we set up a true harmony between the thinking that is freeing itself in the head and the will that is becoming free in the limbs? If we would be educators in the true sense, we must have neither a one-sided regard to thinking nor a one-sided regard to willing, but we must regard the whole being, in all its aspects. This we cannot do with the associated ideas to which we are accustomed when we speak of the spirit to-day; it is only possible to do it when we feel the thinking dominating the present age—as I indicated in my first lecture and again yesterday—as the corpse of living thinking, and feel that we must work our way through to this living thinking by self-development.

In this connection let me here place frankly before you one fundamental principle of all educational reform. I must ask your forbearance if I state this truth quite frankly, because to utter it seems almost like an insult to modern humanity, and one is always reluctant to be insulting. It is a peculiarity of present-day civilization that people know that education must be different. Hence the innumerable unions for educational reform. People know quite well that education is not right and that it ought to be changed; but they are just as firmly convinced that they know very well indeed what education ought to be, that each one in his union can say how one ought to educate. But they should consider this: If education is so bad that it must be fundamentally reformed, they themselves have suffered from it and this bad education has not necessarily made them capable of knowing what a right education is. To-day, every man knows that he and his contemporaries have been badly educated, but he equally assumes that he knows perfectly well what really good education ought to be! And so the educational unions spring up like so many mushrooms.

The Waldorf School method did not take its start from this principle, but from the principle that men do not yet know what education ought to be, and that before anything else one must acquire a fundamental knowledge of the human being. Therefore the first seminary course for the Waldorf

School contained fundamental teaching concerning the being and nature of man, in order that the teachers might gradually learn what they could not yet know—namely, how children ought to be educated. For it is only possible to know how to educate when one understands the real being of man.

The first thing that was imparted to the teachers of the Waldorf School in the seminary course was a fundamental knowledge of man. It was hoped that thus they would gain inner enthusiasm and love for education by contemplating the true nature of man. For when one knows man, the very best thing for the practice of education is the spontaneous love for man that springs up in one. Pedagogy is love for man resulting from knowledge of man—at all events it is only on this foundation that it can be built up.

Now to one who observes human life as expressed in present-day civilization in an external way, all the educational unions will be an outer sign that people know a great deal nowadays about how children ought to be educated. To one who has a deeper perception of human life, it is not so. The Greeks educated by instinct; they did not talk very much about education. Plato was the first who spoke a little, not very much, about education from the standpoint of a kind of philosophical mis-education.

It was not until the sixteenth century that people began to talk a great deal about education. As a matter of fact people as a rule speak very little of what they can do and much more of what they cannot! To one possessed of a deeper knowledge of human nature, a great deal of talk about any subject is not a sign that it is understood; on the contrary, human life reveals to him that when in any age there is a tendency to discuss some subject very much, this is a sign that very little is known about it. And so for one who can truly see into modern civilization, the emergence of the problem of education lies in the fact that no longer is it known how the development of man takes place.

In making a statement like this one must of course ask pardon, and this I do, with all due respect. Truth, however, cannot be concealed; it must be stated. If the Waldorf

School method achieves something, it will achieve it by substituting for ignorance of the human being knowledge of the human being, by substituting for mere external anthropological talk about man, a true anthroposophical insight into his inner nature. And this is the bringing of the living spirit right down into the bodily constitution, the bodily functions.

Some time in the future it will be just as natural to speak of the human being with knowledge as it is mostly natural nowadays to speak with ignorance. Some day it will be known, even in general civilization, how thinking is connected with the force which enables the teeth to grow. Some day people will be able to observe how the inner force of feeling is connected with that which comes from the chest organs and is expressed in the movement of the lips. The change in the lip movements and the control of them by feeling which sets in between the seventh and fourteenth year will be an outer significant sign of an inner development of the human being. It will be observed how the consolidation of the forces flowing from below upwards, which occurs in the human being between the ages of fourteen and twenty-one, takes place and is checked in the human head itself. Just as the quality of thought is made manifest in the teeth and that which comes from feeling in the lips, so a true knowledge of man will see in the highly significant organism of the palate which bounds the cavity of the mouth at the back, the way in which the upward-flowing forces work and, arrested by the gums, pass over into speech. If at some future time people do not only look through the microscope or the telescope when they want to see the most minute or the greatest, but observe all that confronts them outwardly in the world—and this they do not see to-day, in spite of microscope and telescope—then they will perceive how thinking lives in the labial sounds, willing in the palatal sounds which particularly influence the tongue, and how through the labial and palatal sounds, speech, like every other function, becomes an expression of the whole human being.

Attempts are made to-day to "read" the lines of the

hand and other external phenomena of this kind. People try to understand human nature from symptoms. These things can only be rightly understood when it is realized that one must seek for the whole human being in what he expresses, when people perceive how speech, which makes man as an individual being into a social being, is in its inner movement and configuration, a reflection of the whole man. Dental sounds, labial sounds, palatal sounds do not exist in speech by accident; they are there because in the dental sounds the head, in the labial sounds the breast system, in the palatal sounds the rest of the being of man wins its way into speech.

Our civilization must therefore learn to speak about the revelation of the whole human being and then the spirit will be brought to the whole man. Then the way will be found from the spirit of man into the most intimate expressions of his being, namely of his *moral* life. And out of this there will proceed the inner impulse for an education such as we need.

. . . .

The most significant document that can reveal to us how different must be our conception of the world and its civilization from that of olden times, is the Gospel of St. John—the deepest and most beautiful document of Greek culture. This marvellous Gospel shows, even in the first line, that we must rise to ideas of quite a different nature, to living ideas, if we would learn from ancient times something for our present age. In the Gospel of St. John, Greek thought and feeling were the vesture for the newly arising Christianity. The first line runs: " In the Beginning was the Word "—in Greek " the Logos." In the feeling we have to-day when we hear the word " Word " there remains nothing at all of what the writer of the Gospel of St. John felt when he wrote " In the Beginning was the Word." The feeble, insignificant meaning we have when we use the word " Word " was certainly not in the mind of the writer of his Gospel when he wrote the line. In this word " Word " lies something quite different. With us, the " word " is a feeble expression of abstract thoughts. The word only appeals to abstract thoughts. To the Greeks the word was still a call to the human will. When a syllable was uttered, the body of a Greek would tingle to express this syllable through his whole being also. The Greek still knew that one does not only express oneself by saying, for example, " It is all one to me." He knew how, when he heard the phrase, " It is all one to me," he tingled to make these corresponding movements (shrugging the shoulders). The word did not only live in the organ of speech but in the whole of man's organism of movement; but humanity has forgotten these things.

If you want to realize how the word—the word that in ancient Greece still summoned forth a gesture—how the word can live through the whole being of man, you should go to the demonstration of eurhythmy next week. It is all only a beginning, really a modest beginning to bring the word into the will once again, to show the human being (on the stage at any rate, even if it is not possible in ordinary life) in such a way that the word actually lives in the movements of his arms and legs. And when we introduce eurhythmy into our schools, it is a humble beginning—and must still be regarded as such to-day—to make the word once more a moving factor in the whole of life.

In Greece there was still quite a different feeling—a feeling that came over from the East. There was a tingling, an urge in the human being to let the will reveal itself through the limbs, with every syllable, with every word, every phrase, with the rhythm and measure of every phrase. He realized how the word could become creative in every movement. But in those days he knew still more. Words were to him expressions for the forces of cloud formation, the forces lying in the growth of plants and all natural phenomena. The word rumbled in the rolling waves, worked in the whistling wind. Just as the word lives in my breath so that I make a corresponding movement, so did the Greek find all that was living in the word in the raging wind, in the surging wave, even in the rumbling earthquake. These were words pouring out of the earth.

The paltry ideas which arise in us when we use the word

"word" would be very much out of place if I were to transfer them to the primal beginning of the world. I wonder what sort of a start we should have made with these words and ideas, if at the beginning of the world these feeble ideas of the "word" had been there, and were supposed to be creative? Our words have become intellectualistic; they no longer have creative power.

Thus, above all things, we must rise to what the Greek felt as a revelation of the whole human being, a call to the will, when he spoke of the Word, of the Logos. The Greek felt the Logos surging and sounding through the whole cosmos. And then he felt what really resounds in the line: "In the Beginning was the Word." In all that was conjured up in these words there lived the living creative force not only within man but in wind and wave, cloud, sunshine and starlight. Everywhere the world and the cosmos were a revelation of the Word. Greek gymnastic was a revelation of the Word. And in its weaker division, in musical education, there was a shadowy image of all that was felt in the Word. The Word worked in Greek wrestling. The shadowy image of the Word in music worked in the Greek dances. The spirit worked into the nature of man even though it was a bodily, gymnastic education that was given.

We must realize how feeble our ideas have become in modern civilization, and come to perceive rightly how the mighty impulse pulsating through such a line as "In the Beginning was the Word" was weakened when it passed over into Roman culture, becoming more and more shadowy, until all we now feel is an inner lassitude when we speak of it. In olden times, all wisdom, all science was a commentary on the sentence "In the Beginning was the Word." At first, the Word, the Logos, lived in the ideas that arose in man when he spoke these words, but this life grew feebler and feebler. And then came the Middle Ages and the Logos died. Only the dead Logos could be tolerated in man. And those who were educated were not only educated by having the dead Logos communicated to them, but also the dead word—the Latin tongue in its decay. The dying word of speech became the chief medium of education up to the time of the sixteenth century, when there arose a certain inner revolt against it.

What then does civilization signify up to the sixteenth century? The death of human feeling for the living Logos as it is contained in the Gospel of St. John. And the actual clinging to a dead language is an outer manifestation of this death of the Logos. If one wanted briefly to characterize the course of civilization in so far as it fundamentally affects the impulses of education, one really should say: All that humanity has lost is expressed most of all in the fact that it has understood less and less of such things as live in the Gospel of St. John.

The course of civilization through the Middle Ages up to the sixteenth century lost the inner force of a writing like the Gospel of St. John, and this has resulted in the lack existing in humanity to-day; hence the clamour for educational reforms. The question of education in our age will only assume its right bearing, when people realize the barrenness of the human heart when it wants to understand the Gospel of St. John, and compares this with the intense devotion which arose in man when he believed himself to be transported from his own being out into all the creative forces of the universe, as he allowed the true content of this first sentence of the Gospel to ring out within him—" In the Beginning was the Word." We must realize that the cry of the sixteenth and seventeenth centuries for a different kind of education arose because the most godly people of that time, those who felt most deeply the need for a renewal of education, also sensed the loss of the inner elementary life-force which enables man also to have a living understanding of the spirit. For it is the spirit to which the Gospel of St. John refers when it speaks of the Logos.

We have reached a point where we do indeed long for the spirit, but our speech is composed of mere words. And in the words we have lost the spirit that still existed for the Greeks, inasmuch as the whole human being in his activity in the world dawned upon them when the word was uttered, just as in still earlier times the activity of the universe dawned upon man when in the world-creative, cosmos-creative words he recognized the Divine that the world rests on and that must become living in man if he is to become a " whole " man. And the teacher must become a whole man, for otherwise he can educate only half men and quarter men. The teacher must again come to an understanding of the Word.

. . . .

If we would bring before our souls this mystery of the Word, the Word in its fulness, as it worked and was understood in the age when the full significance of the Gospel of St. John was still felt, we must say to ourselves: In the old consciousness of man, spirit was present in the word—even in the feeble word that was used in speech. Spirit poured into the word and was the power within it.

I am not criticizing any epoch, nor do I say that one epoch is of less value than another. I merely want to describe how the different epochs follow one another, each having its special value. But some epochs have to be characterized more by negative, some more by positive characteristics.

Let us picture to ourselves the darkness, the dimness that gradually crept over the living impulse in the word when the sentence "In the Beginning was the Word" was spoken. Let us now consider civilized mankind in the sixteenth or seventeenth centuries, and how they had to prepare for a growth of the inner force of freedom. You see one has also to value elements that were not present in certain periods; indeed, from a certain point of view, to value them rightly for the first time. Consider, then, that humanity had to win its freedom with full consciousness and this would not have been possible if the spirit had still poured into and inspired the word as in earlier times. Then we shall understand how education in its old form became an impossibility, as soon as Francis Bacon of Verulam, in the sixteenth and seventeenth centuries, came forward with a significant statement which, when we face it honestly, implies an annihilation of what is contained in the phrase " In the Beginning was the Word."

Before this time there was always a shadow of the spirit in the Word, in the Logos. Bacon asks mankind to see in the word only an idol, no longer the spirit but the idol, no longer to hold fast by the word with its own power but to guard against the "intellectualism" of the word. For if one has lost the real content of the word out of which, in earlier times, knowledge, civilization and power were drawn, one is clinging to an idol—so thinks Bacon of Verulam. In the doctrine of idols which appears with Bacon of Verulam lies the whole change at the epoch of the sixteenth and seventeenth centuries, away from the word. Whither does man tend? Towards the things of sense. The things perceptible to the senses—this it was which should underlie that to which man was taught to hold fast.

Thus there was once an age when man not only received the word in the word but also the spirit, indeed the world-creative spirit living in the Word, in the Logos. Then came the age when the word became an idol, a misleading thing, an idol that misleads one into intellectualism. Man was taught to hold fast by the outer, sensible object lest he fall a prey to the idol in the word. Bacon of Verulam demands that man shall not now hold fast to that which pours into him from the Gods—but to that which lies in the outer world in lifeless objects—or at most in externally enlivened objects. Man is directed away from the Word to outer sensible objects. This feeling alone remains in him: he must educate, he must approach the human being, in whom indeed the spirit is present; but the word is an idol. He can only direct the human being to look with his eyes at what is external, outside man. Education no longer makes use of what is truly human but of what is outside the human.

And now there arises the problem of education, bringing fierce zeal but also fearful tragedy in the form we have it with us to-day. We see it very characteristically in the sixteenth and seventeenth centuries in Michel de Montaigne, in John Locke and—parallel with what was happening here in England—we see it in Comenius over on the Continent. In these three men, Montaigne, Locke, Comenius, we can approximately see how the departure from the Logos, and the turning towards sensible objects becomes the strongest impulse in civilization. Fear of the idol in the word arose in men. The Logos disappears. What is called observation, a function which is quite justifiable—as we shall see in the following lectures—but which is now understood to mean sense observation, becomes the decisive factor. And we see how anxiously Montaigne, how John Locke and Comenius desire to divert man from all that is supersensible, all that is living in the Logos. John Locke and Comenius always point to what is outside the human being and try expressly to avoid all that is not the direct object of the senses, to bring as much of the sense-world as possible to the young through education. We see Comenius writing books, the object of which is to show that one ought not to work through the word but through artificially created sense-perceptions. We see how the transition is accomplished, how mankind loses the feeling of all connection with the spirit through the word. We see how civilisation as a whole can no longer inwardly accept something like "In the Beginning was the Word," but how mankind clamps civilisation to the outer facts of sense, and how the Word, the Logos, is only accepted still because it has become tradition.

Thus the longing arises—with intense zeal but also with fearful tragedy—only to educate by means of sense-perception, because the Word is felt to be an idol in the Baconian sense. And this longing appears in its most symptomatic form in Montaigne, John Locke and Comenius. They, however, in their turn, show us—from their eminence—what is living in the whole of humanity; they show us how the mood which finds expression to-day as our deep longing to bring the spirit once again to the human being, arose just when men could no longer believe in the spirit any more but only in the idol of the word, as did Bacon of Verulam. From that which has lived in all educational unions up to the present day, beginning with Montaigne and Amos Comenius —fully justified as it was in those times—there must develop for the sake of the present age something which is able to bring the spirit to man, the spirit which has been given form, which has been experienced and bears forces of will, something which can recognize in the body of man and in his earthly deeds a revelation of that spirit which reveals itself in supersensible worlds.

With this supersensible within the sensible, with this rediscovery of the spirit which has been lost in the Word, in the Logos, since the Word became an idol, with this rediscovery of the spirit begins the new era of education. Montaigne, John Locke and Comenius knew very well what education ought to be. Their programmes are just as splendid as those of modern educational unions, and all that people demand for education to-day is already to be found in abstract paragraphs in the writings of these three. What we have to find to-day, however, are the means which will lead us to reality. For no education will develop from abstract principles or programmes—it will only develop from reality. And because man himself is soul and spirit, because he has a physical nature, a soul nature and a spiritual nature, reality must again come into our life—for with the whole reality will the spirit also come into our life, and only such a spirit as this can sustain the educational art of the future.

VI

WALKING, SPEAKING, THINKING

The previous lectures have in no way attempted to formulate new educational theories, but to create a true feeling for education. My aim has been to speak to the human heart rather than to the intellect. This is all important, all essential for the teacher because, as we have seen, the art of education must develop from a deeper knowledge of man's whole being.

For a long time now it has been usual to hear in educational circles that this or that should be done in teaching. Very frequently the training of teachers consists of little beyond the assimilation of certain rules and theories as to the treatment of the child. The full devotion of the teacher to his task will never be brought forth in this way: it will only be brought forth if he is really able to penetrate into the whole nature of man as body, soul and spirit. In one who has living ideas about man in this way and who is then engaged in his calling, these living ideas become immediate will. He learns from hour to hour to find practical answers to important questions. Who puts these questions? It is the child himself. And so the most important thing is to learn to read in the child. And a real and practical knowledge of man in body, soul and spirit makes it possible really to learn to read in the child.

It is for this reason difficult to describe the education given at the Waldorf School. It is not a thing that can be " learnt " or discussed; it is purely and simply a matter of practice, and one can only give examples of a practical way of dealing with the needs of particular cases. Such practice must be the outcome of actual experience, for knowledge of human nature is naturally a *sine qua non* in this way of working. Education is a social concern in the widest possible sense, for it begins immediately after birth. It is the concern of each individual family and community, indeed of the whole of humanity. This is brought home to us in the strongest way of all by a knowledge of the child's nature before the change of teeth at about the seventh year. A German writer—Jean Paul Friedrich Richter—spoke words of great truth when he said that in the first three years of life a man learns more than in all his subsequent student years. (In his time there were only three.)

The first three years, and from then onwards to the seventh year, are much the most important in the whole development of a man, for the child is not at all the same being as in later life. In his earliest years the child is one great sense-organ. The scope of this idea that the child in its first years is wholly sense-organ is not generally brought to mind with anything like sufficient intensity; indeed it is a question of using very emphatic words if the whole truth is to be expressed.

In later years, for instance, man tastes his food in his mouth, on his gums and tongue. Taste is localized, so to say, in the head. But with the child, and especially during these early years, this is not the case. Taste then works throughout the whole organism; the child tastes its mother's milk, its first food, right down into its very limbs. The processes that in later life take place in the tongue, extend over the whole organism in the young child, who lives, as it were, in that it tastes all that it takes in. There is a strong element of animality here, but we must never compare this element in the child with the ordinary animal nature. The animal nature in the child is always raised, so to say, on to a higher level. The human being is never an animal, not even in the embryonic state—in fact, at that period least of all. But one can clarify ideas by putting them in such a way, by using a comparison.

Those who have a true insight into the processes of nature, may have the following impression of these processes in the animal, if they look at a herd of cows grazing in a meadow.

As each cow lies down to digest its food, it gives itself up in a most wonderful way to the cosmos. A whole world, an entire extract of the cosmic process is at work in the digesting animal, which experiences the most marvellous visions. The digesting process in the animal is a mighty act of knowledge. While it digests it is given up to the cosmos in an imaginative, dreamlike way. This may seem an extravagant statement, yet strange to say, it is absolutely true.

If we now raise this process one stage higher, we can understand how the child experiences the functions of its bodily organism. All these physical functions are accompanied by a kind of tasting; and, moreover, the other processes that in later life are localized in eye and ear, also extend over the whole organism of the child.

Think of the wonders of the eye—of how the eye takes in colour from outside and makes an inner picture. This process is localized, separated off from our conscious experience of life as a whole. The intellect takes hold of what the eye forms in so wonderful a way and makes of it a shadowy, mental image. Equally wonderful are those processes which, in the adult, are localized in the ear. All that is localized in the several senses of the adult is spread out over the whole organism in the child. Accordingly in the child there is no separation between spirit, soul, and body. Everything from without is reproduced in his inner being. He imitates his whole environment.

And now, bearing this in mind, we must observe how three faculties, conditioning the whole of life, are acquired by the child during his earliest years—the faculties of walking, speaking, and thinking.

" To walk " is, so to say, only an abbreviation for something far, far greater. We say that the child learns to walk because this is the most evident feature of the process. But this learning to walk is the bringing of man into a right equilibrium in the whole world of space. As children, we strive for the upright posture, to relate our legs to the laws of gravity in a way that will give balance—we do the same with the arms and hands. The whole organism is orientated.

Learning to walk means to find, to place the organism into, the directions of space. Here we must rightly regard the fact that the child is an imitative sense-being; for everything during the first years of life must be learnt through imitation, must be won through imitation from the environment. Now it is evident that the organism sends forth the powers of orientation out of itself, and that it is adapted from the beginning to attain the vertical and not to remain in the crawling, the horizontal position, to use the arms correspondingly for the maintenance of balance in space. All this inheres in the very nature of the child and is brought about by the impulses of the organism itself.

If we now begin as educators to bring coercion to bear on what human nature itself wills to do, if we do not understand how to leave this nature to itself in freedom and act only as helpers ourselves, we injure the organism of the child for the whole of its later earthly life. If we wrongly force the child to walk by external methods, if we do not merely help but urge him to walk or to stand, we do the child an injury which lasts till death and is especially harmful in advanced age. In true methods of education it can never be a question of considering the child as it is at a given mnment, but in the relation to the whole of its journey through life from birth to death; for the seed of the whole earthly life is already present from the first.

Now because the child is a most delicately balanced organ of sense, he is not only sensitive to the physical influences of his surroundings, but also to the moral influences, especially those of thought. However far-fetched it may appear to the modern materialistic mind, the child does, nevertheless, sense all that those in his environment are thinking. As parents or teachers we must not only refrain from actions that are outwardly unseemly, but we must be inwardly true, inwardly moral in our thought and feeling, for the child senses these things and absorbs them. He does not merely shape his nature according to our words and actions, but in accordance with our whole attitude of heart and mind. The environment, then, is the most important thing of all in the first period of the child's education—up to the seventh year.

And now the question will arise: What kind of help are we to give in this process of orientation and learning to walk? Here it must be remembered that the connecting threads of life can be observed by a science that is spiritual in character, but not by a science that is materialistic and dead.

Let us take a child who has been forced on to walk and to adjust himself in space by all kinds of coercive measures, and then look at him in his fiftieth year, or between the fifties and sixties. If nothing else has intervened, we shall find him suffering from all manner of metabolic diseases which he cannot throw off; from rheumatism, gout, and so on. Everything of the nature of soul and spirit that we do to the child—for we are exercising forces of the soul and spirit if we urge him to adopt the vertical position, or to walk, even if we do so in unconcerned ignorance—everything reaches the stage where the spiritual works right down into the physical. And the forces remain. The forces that have been called into play by the use of highly questionable methods remain for the whole of the earthly life, and reappear later in the form of bodily diseases.

It is just with children that all education is at the same time physical education. We cannot educate children merely physically, for all that is of soul and spirit in education works at the same time upon the physical, is indeed physical education. When we observe how the child's organism adjusts itself to attain the upright position, and to walk, and we lovingly watch this wonderful mystery enacted by the human organism as it passes from the horizontal to the vertical position; when out of religious feeling we approach the child with reverence for the creative, divine powers which are placing him rightly into space; when, in other words, we are there as helpers of the child in its learning to walk and balance itself, as helpers who inwardly love the human nature in the child, who follow every manifestation of this human nature with love, then we generate health-bringing forces which can then re-appear as healthy metabolic activities between the ages of fifty and sixty, a time of life when we especially need control of the processes of metabolism.

Herein lies truly the mystery of human evolution: *All that is of the nature of soul and spirit at one stage of life becomes physical—manifests itself physically in later life.* Years later it makes itself evident in the physical body.

So much, then, for learning to walk. A child who is lovingly guided to walk develops into a healthy man, and to apply this love in the process of learning to walk is to add much to the healthy education of the body.

Now speech develops from this process of orientation in space. Modern physiology knows something of this, but not very much. It knows that the movements of the right hand correspond to a certain activity of the left side of the brain, which is related to speech. Physiology admits the correspondence between the right-hand movements and the so-called convolution of Broca at the left side of the brain. The hand moves, makes gestures; forces pour into it, pass into the brain, where they become the impulse of speech. Science knows only a fragment of the process, for the truth is this: Speech does not arise merely because a movement of the right hand coincides with a convolution in the left portion of the brain; speech arises from the entire motor-organism of the human being. How the child learns to walk, to orientate himself in space, to transmute the first erratic and uncontrolled movements of the arms into gestures definitely related to the outer world—all this is carried over by the mysterious processes of the human organism to the head, and manifests as speech.

Anyone who is able to understand these things, realizes that children who shuffle their feet at they walk pronounce every sound, and especially the palate sounds, quite differently from those whose gait is firm. Every nuance of speech is derived from the organization of movement; life to begin with is all gestures, and gesture is inwardly transformed into speech.

Speaking, then, is an outcome of walking—that is to say, of orientation in space. And the degree to which the child is able to control speech will depend very largely upon whether we give him loving help while he is learning to walk.

These are some of the finer connections revealed by a true knowledge of man. Not without reason have I described in detail the process of bringing the spirit to the human organism. Thus one brings the spirit to the body; for with every step that is taken, the body follows the spirit, if the spirit is brought to the child in the right way.

Again, it is a fact that, to begin with, the whole organism is active when the child is learning to speak. First there are the outer movements, the movements of the legs—these produce the strong contours of speech; the more delicate movements of the arms and hands determine the inflection and plastic form of the words. In short, outer movements are transformed into the inner movements of speech.

Just as the element of love should pervade the help we give to the child as he learns to walk, so as we help him to speak we must also be inwardly true. The greatest untruthfulness of all in after life is generated during the time when a child is learning to speak, for in those years the element of truth in speech is absorbed by the whole bodily organism. A child whose teachers are filled with inner truthfulness will, as he imitates his environment, so learn to speak that the subtle activity constantly generated in the organism by the processes of in-breathing and out-breathing will be strengthened. Naturally, these things must be understood in a delicate and not in a crude sense. The processes are indeed delicate, but are nevertheless revealed in every manifestation of life. We breathe in oxygen and exhale carbonic acid. Oxygen has to be changed into carbonic acid in the body by the breathing process. We receive oxygen from the cosmos, and give back carbonic acid. Truth or untruthfulness in those around us while we are learning to speak determines whether, in the more subtle functions of life, we are able to change the oxygen within us into carbonic acid in the right way. This process is a complete transmutation of the spiritual into the physical.

One of the most common and untruthful influences brought to the child is the use of "baby-language." Unconsciously the child does not like this; he wants to listen to true speech, the speech of grown men and women. We should speak in ordinary language to the child and avoid the use of this "baby-language." At first the child will naturally only babble in imitation of words, but we ourselves must not copy this babbling. For that is the greatest mistake. To use to the child its own babbling, imperfect speech is to injure his digestive organs. Once more the spiritual becomes physical, and works directly into the bodily organs. And all that we do spiritually near the child is also a physical training. Many later defects in the digestive system are caused by a child having learnt to speak in a wrong way.

Just as speech arises from walking and grasping, in short from movement, so thought develops from speech. In helping the child as he learns to walk we must be pervaded by love; in helping the child to gain the power of speech we must be absolutely truthful, and since the child is one great sense organ and in his inner physical functions also copies the spiritual, our own thinking must be clear if right thinking is to develop in the child from the forces of speech.

No greater harm can be done to the child than by the giving of orders, and then causing confusion by reversing them. Confusion that exists in the child's surroundings as the result of inconsequent thinking is the actual root of the many so-called nervous diseases prevalent in our modern civilization.

Why have so many people "nerves" to-day? Simply because in childhood there was no clarity and precision of thought around them during the time when they were learning to think after having learnt to speak. The physical condition of the next generation, as evinced by its gravest defects, is a faithful copy of the preceding generation. When we observe the faults in our children which develop in later life, we should be prompted to a little self-knowledge. All that happens in the child's environment expresses itself in the physical organism—though in a subtle and delicate sense. Loving treatment while the child is learning to walk, truthfulness while he learns to speak, clarity and precision as he begins to be able to think—all these qualities become a part of the bodily constitution. The organs and vessels develop after the models of love, truth, and clarity. Diseases of the metabolic system are the result of unkind treatment while the child is learning to walk. Digestive disturbances may arise from untruthful actions during the time the child is beginning to speak. Nerve trouble is the outcome of confused thinking in the child's environment.

When we see the prevalence of nervous disease in this third decade of the twentieth century, we cannot but conclude that there must have been much confused thinking on the part of the educators about the beginning of the century. Many diseases of the nerves to-day are really due to confused thinking, and again, the nerve troubles from which people suffered at the beginning of the century were equally the result of the confused thought of the last three decades of the nineteenth century.

Now these matters can be handled in such a way that physiology, hygiene, and psychology no longer need to remain shut off from each other as specialized branches of knowledge, so that to-day the teacher must call in the doctor the moment any question of health arises. Physiological education, school hygiene, and the like, can be so united, that then the teacher's spiritual mission will come to include an understanding of the activity of the soul and spirit in the physical organism. But since everyone has, in a certain sense, to educate children from birth up to the seventh year, a social task stands before us, inasmuch as a true knowledge of man is necessary for all if humanity is to follow an ascending, and not a descending, path.

. . . .

Quite rightly has our humane age attempted to do away with a certain educational measure very frequently applied in earlier days—I mean that of caning. The last thing I wish to do is to speak in favour of such punishment, but it is just because our age has a good eye for externals that it is getting rid of it; it is well able to recognize the physical and moral harm arising from it. Just in this age too, however, when all eyes are so concentrated on the physical and external and there is so little understanding for the soul and spirit, a terrible form of punishment has crept in, a way of beating the child which is never realized as such, because men's minds are too little directed to the spirit.

Parents often think it desirable to give their little girl a beautiful doll as a plaything. This " beautiful " doll is a fearful production, because, for one thing, it is so utterly inartistic, in spite of its " real " hair, painted cheeks and eyes that close when it is laid down or lifted up! We often give our children toys that are dreadfully inartistic so-called copies of life—the doll is merely one example. All modern toys are tending to be of the same type, and they represent a form of cruel punishment to the child's inner nature. Even when punished children often behave well in the presence of others simply because convention demands it; equally out of politeness they do not always express aversion towards toys like the " beautiful doll," although this dislike is deeply rooted in their souls. However strongly we may suggest to children that they ought to love such toys—the forces of their unconscious and subconscious life are stronger, and they have an intense antipathy to anything resembling the beautiful doll. For, as I will now show you, such toys really amount to an inner punishment.

Suppose that in the making of our toys we were to take into consideration what the child has actually experienced in his infant thought up to the age of six or seven, in the process of learning to stand upright and to walk—and then we were to make a doll out of a handkerchief, for instance, showing a head at the top with two ink-spots for eyes. The child can understand and, moreover, really love such a doll. Primitively, this doll possesses all the qualities of the human form, in so far at any rate as the child is capable of observing them at this early age. A child knows no more about the human being than that he stands upright, that there is an " upper " and a " lower " part of his being, that he has a head and a pair of eyes. As for the mouth, you will often find it on the forehead in a child's drawings! There is as yet no clear consciousness of the exact position of the mouth.

What a child actually experiences is all contained in a doll made from a handkerchief with a couple of ink-spots for eyes. An inner, plastic force is at work in the child. All that comes to him from the environment passes over into his being and there becomes an inner formative power, a power that also builds up the organs of the body.

If the child, for example, has a father who is constantly ill-tempered and irritable, and as a result of this the child lives in an environment of perpetual shocks and unreasonableness, all this turmoil expresses itself in his breathing and the circulation of the blood. This means, however, that the lungs, heart, and the whole vascular system are affected by such a condition. Through the whole of his life the child bears plastically formed within him the inner effects of seeing his father's ill-temper.

This is merely an example to show you that the child possesses a wonderful plastic power and is perpetually at work as a kind of inner sculptor upon his own being. If we give the child the kind of doll made from a handkerchief, these plastic, creative forces that arise in the human organism —especially from the rhythmic system of the breathing and blood circulation—and build up the brain, flow gently upwards to the brain. They mould the brain like a sculptor who works upon his material with a fine and supple hand— a hand permeated with the forces of the soul and spirit. Everything here is in a formative process, in organic development. The child looks at the handkerchief-doll and that becomes formative force, real formative force, which then flows upwards from the rhythmic system and works upon the structure of the brain.

If, on the contrary, we give the child one of the so-called " beautiful " dolls which can move, which has moving eyes and painted cheeks, real hair, and so on—a hideous, ghostly production from the artistic point of view—then the plastic, brain-building forces that are generated in the rhythmic system have the effect of constant lashes of a whip. The child cannot as yet understand these things and it is as though the brain were enduring the lashings of a whip. The brain is thoroughly whipped, thoroughly flogged in a fearful way.

Such is the secret of the "beautiful" doll, and it can be applied to many of the playthings given to the child to-day.

If we would give loving help to the child at play we must realize how many inner, formative forces are active in his being. In this respect our whole civilization is on the wrong road. For instance, modern culture has evolved the concept of "animism." A child bumps against the table, and strikes it in anger. We say to-day that the child credits the table with life, imagines it to be alive, dreams life into it, and strikes it. Now this is not true. The child dreams nothing at all into the table, but he dreams life out of what is really alive. When he hurts himself, a kind of reflex movement makes him hit the table. And since everything is without life for the child, he treats the living and the lifeless in exactly the same way.

These topsy-turvy ideas show that our civilization simply does not know how to approach children. The first great essential is to learn to deal with them lovingly, and lovingly give them only what their own being demands. We should not inflict inner punishments by giving the child toys of the type of the beautiful doll. We should be able to live with him, and fashion dolls which he himself can inwardly experience.

Thus play also is something that calls for true insight into the nature of the child. If we prattle like small infants and think to bring our speech down to his level, if we do not speak in the genuine way in which the child must hear our speech coming from us, we bring an untruthful influence to bear upon the child. On the other hand, however, we must be able to descend to the stage of the child's development in everything that has to do with the will-nature in everything that goes into his play. We shall then realize that intellectuality—a quality so much admired in this age—simply does not exist in the child's organic nature, and should therefore have no place in his play.

The child at play will naturally imitate what is going on in his surroundings, but it will seldom happen that a child of four expresses a wish to be, let us say, a philologist, although he may say he would like to be a chauffeur! Why? Because everything about a chauffeur can be seen. It makes a direct pictorial impression. It is different with a philologist, for what he does makes no such impression; it is unpictorial, it simply passes by unnoticed by the child. In play, however, we must introduce only what does not pass by the child unnoticed. Everything intellectual leaves the child unaffected, it passes him by. What, then, must we adults do if we are to help the child to the right kind of play?

Now when we plough, or make hats, or sew clothes, and so on, all these things are done with a certain purpose, and in this purposiveness the intellectual element lies. When we discern the purpose of a thing in life, we penetrate it intellectually. But everything in life—no matter whether it be ploughing, building carriages, shoeing horses, or the like—besides having a definite purpose, contains another element in outward appearance, its mere outward appearance. At the sight of a man guiding his plough over the field, one can feel—apart from the object of ploughing—what one might call the plastic quality of the picture, of what becomes a picture. If we struggle through to a feeling for this pictorial, formative element—quite apart from its purpose—(and it is the aesthetic sense that enables us to do this)—then we can begin to make toys that really appeal to the child. We shall not aim at intellectual beauty (as in the modern doll), but at something expressed in the whole movement, in the whole feeling of the human being. Then, instead of the beautiful doll, we shall produce for the older children a primitive, really enchanting doll something like this one.*

In true education, therefore, the essential thing is to be able to bring an artistic element into our work. If we apply it in the making of toys, we then begin to satisfy what is willed by the child's own nature.

Our civilization has made us, with very few exceptions, wholly utilitarian, intellectualistic, and we offer even our children the result of what we have " thought out " with our

* Dr. Steiner here showed a doll made by pupils of the Waldorf School.

brains. But we ought not to give them what adult life has so thought out, but what our maturer life feels and perceives. This is the quality the toy ought to exhibit. If we give a child a toy plough, the essential thing is that it should express the aesthetic quality in ploughing, for this will help to unfold the full forces of the human being.

Certain Kindergarten systems—in other ways worthy of all respect—have made great mistakes in this connection. Froebel's system, as also others, have arisen from a true inner love for children, but they have failed to realize that although imitation is a part of the very nature of the child, he can only imitate that which is not yet permeated by an intellectual quality. We must therefore not introduce into the Kindergarten such various forms of handwork as have been ingeniously " thought out." The arranging of sticks, basket-work and so on, that play so large a part in modern Kindergarten methods, have all been ingeniously thought out. Kindergarten work ought rather to be so arranged that it contains an actual picture of what older people do, and not mere inventions. A sense of tragedy will often arise in one possessed of a true knowledge of man when he goes into these modern Kindergartens—for they are so full of good intentions and the work has been so conscientiously thought out. They are based on infinite goodwill and a sincere love of children, yet on the other hand it has not been realized that all intellectualism, all that has just been thought out, ought to be eliminated. Kindergarten work should consist simply and solely of the external imitation of the external picture of what grown-up people do.

A child whose intellectual faculties are developed before the fourth or fifth year bears a dreadful heritage into later life. He will simply become a materialist. To the extent that an intellectual education is given to the child before the fourth or fifth year will he become materialistic in later life. For the brain is so worked on that the intellectually spiritual takes hold of it, lives in its forms, and the human being, because this process has taken place too soon, comes to the view that everything is just material.

If we would so train the child that as man he may comprehend the spirit, we must delay as long as possible the giving of the outwardly spiritual in a purely intellectual form. Although it is highly necessary, in view of the nature of our modern civilization, that a man should be fully awake in later life, the child must be allowed to remain as long as possible in the peaceful, dreamlike condition of pictorial imagination in which his early years are passed. For if we allow his organism to grow strong in this non-intellectual way, he will rightly develop in later life the intellectuality needed in the world to-day.

If the child's brain has been flogged in the way I have described, permanent injury is done to the soul. Just as the use of baby-language injuriously affects the digestion and unloving, mistaken coercion in the process of learning to walk has an unfavourable effect upon the metabolic system in later life, so the flogging of the child in this way from within harms the soul. It must be the first aim of education to do away with this punishment of the soul which, because the child is body, soul and spirit throughout its being, also, from within, harms the body; we must do away with the beautiful doll, and make it a first aim to bring the play of children on to its proper level.

In these lectures I have tried to indicate how false forms of spirituality must be avoided when we are dealing with the child, so that a true spirituality—in short, the whole man—may come to full expression in later life.

VII

THE RHYTHMIC SYSTEM, SLEEPING AND WAKING, IMITATION

The transition from early childhood to the school age is marked by the change of teeth at about the seventh year, and in studying this period it must above all be remembered that up to the seventh year the child is working, as it were, as an inner sculptor. The formative forces go out from the head, organizing and moulding his whole being. All that has been present in his environment, including the moral qualities, now plays a part in the development of the vascular system, the circulation of the blood and the processes of the breath, so that as a physical being man bears within him throughout his earthly life the results of the imitative period of his childhood from birth up to the time of the second dentition.

It cannot, of course, be said that he is conditioned only by this, for naturally much can be rectified in the body later by the exercise of moral forces and inner activity of soul. Still, we should realize with what a wonderful heritage we can endow the child on his path of life, if we make his physical organism into a bearer of moral, spiritual qualities—if, in other words, we help the sculptor within him up to the age of seven by bringing near to him only what is moral and conducive to fruitful activity in life.

I spoke more in detail about these things yesterday, and much else will emerge as the lectures proceed.

The teacher, then, must understand that when the child has passed his seventh year these plastic forces are transformed into an activity in the soul, so that the child longs for pictures, imagery, and this fact should indicate to us the fundamental principle of his education.

From the time of the second dentition to the age of adolescence, the development of the rhythmic system—*i.e.*, the breathing and the circulation of the blood, together with all that belongs to the regular rhythm of the digestive functions, is all-important. Whereas the teacher finds the need for pictorial imagery in the soul of the child, he has to deal with the rhythmic system as an organic bodily thing. For this reason, a pictorial, imaginative element must prevail in all that the child is given to do; a musical quality, I might even say, must pervade the relationship between teacher and pupil. Rhythm, measure, even melody must be there as the basic principle of the teaching, and this demands that the teacher have this musical quality in himself, in his whole life.

It is the rhythmic system that predominates in the child's organic nature during this first period of school life, and the entire teaching must follow a certain rhythm. The teacher must have this musical element so deeply—and in a certain way instinctively—in him, that true rhythm may prevail in the classroom.

It thus becomes evident that during the early years of school life (that is to say after the age of seven) all true education must develop from the foundation of art. The reason why education in our day leaves so much to be desired is because modern civilization is not conducive to the development of artistic feeling. I am not here referring to the individual arts, but to the fact that sound educational principles can only develop from an entirely artistic conception of civilization. This has very great significance.

If we can imbue our whole teaching with an artistic quality, we influence the rhythmic system in the child. Such lessons actually make the child's breathing and circulation more healthy. We must be clear too that, on the one hand, our task is also to lead the child out into life, to develop a sound faculty of judgment for later life, and so during this age we must teach him to use his intelligence, though never by any coercion. On the other hand, we must help the child to be healthy in later life, in so far as his destiny permits, and so we must give proper attention to the care and exercise of the body. But to accomplish all this we need a deeper insight into the whole nature of man.

In our modern civilization, where all eyes are concentrated on outer, material things, no attention is given to the consideration of the state of sleep, although man devotes to it one-third of his earthly life. This alternating rhythm of our waking and sleeping is of the greatest possible significance. Never should it be thought that man is inactive while he sleeps. He is inactive only in so far as the outer external world is concerned, but as regards the health of his body, and more especially the health of his soul and spirit, sleep is all-important. True education can provide for a right life of sleep, for whatever activities belong to man's waking hours are carried over into the condition of sleep, and this is especially the case with the child.

We must only understand this fact, that the rhythmic system, which lies at the basis of all artistic activity, never grows tired. Breathing and the action of the heart continue from birth to death. It is only the processes of thought and will that induce fatigue. Thinking and movement of the body cause fatigue, and since they everywhere come into play, we may say that all life's activities cause fatigue. But in the case of the child we must be especially watchful that this happens as little as possible. We do this if we see to it that throughout the all-important early school years our teaching has a basic artistic quality, for we then call upon the child's rhythmic system, where he tires least of all.

What, then, will happen if we make too great a demand on the intellect, urging the child to think, into thinking as such? Certain organic forces that tend inwardly to harden the body are brought into play. These forces are responsible for the salty deposits in the body and for the formation of bone, cartilage and sinew—in all those parts of the body, in short, that have a tendency to become rigid. This normal rigidity is over-developed if intellectual thinking is forced. The human being is inwardly at work on the hardening of his organism when he is awake, and this activity is overdone if we make undue claims upon the intellect. If we force the child to think too much, we are sowing the seed of premature arterial sclerosis.

Thus here, too, it is essential to develop, by means of a true observation of the nature of the child, a fine sense of how much we may demand of him. A most vital principle is here at stake. If I allow the child to think, if I teach him to write, for instance, in an intellectual way, saying: " Here are the letters and you must learn them," I am over-straining the mental powers of the child and laying the germs of sclerosis—at any rate of a tendency to sclerosis. The human being, as such, has no inner relationship whatever to the letters of modern script. They are little " demons " so far as human nature is concerned, and we have to find the right way to approach them. This way, this transition, is found if, to begin with, we engaged the child's artistic feeling by letting him paint or draw the lines and colours that flow of themselves on to the paper from his innermost being. Then, when the child is artistically active in this way, one always feels—and feeling is here the essential thing—how man is too much enriched by this artistic activity. One feels that intellectuality impoverishes the soul, makes a man inwardly barren, whereas artistic activity makes him inwardly rich—so rich, in fact, that this richness must somehow be modified. The pictorial and artistic tends of itself to pass into the more attenuated form of concepts and ideas; the need arises to impoverish the artistic, to intellectualize it. But if, after having stimulated the child artistically, we then allow the intellectuality to develop from the artistic feeling, this artistic element will have the right intensity. It will lay hold of the body in such a way that a rightly balanced, and not an excessive hardening takes place.

If we force intellectual powers in the child we arrest growth; but we liberate the forces of growth if we approach the intellect by way of art. For this reason, at the Waldorf School, value is placed upon artistic rather than intellectual training at the beginning of school life. The teaching is at first pictorial, non-intellectual; the relation of the teacher to the child is pervaded by a musical, rhythmic quality, and by such methods we achieve the degree of intellectual development that the child needs. The mental training in this way becomes, at the same time, the very best training for the physical body.

To the more sensitive observer, there is abundant evidence in our present civilization that many grown-up people are too inwardly rigid. They seem to drag their bodies around like wooden machines. It is really a characteristic of our day that men and women carry their bodies about like burdens, whereas a truer and more artistically conceived educational system so develops the human being that every step, every gesture of the hand to be devoted later to the service of humanity, gives him an inner sense of joy and well-being. If we educate intellectually we loosen the soul from the body, so that the human being will go through life feeling that his body is " of the earth earthy," that it is of no value and must be overcome. Then he may give himself up to a purely mystical life of soul and spirit, feeling that the spirit alone has value. Right education, however, also leads us by ways of truth to the spirit, that is, to the body-creative spirit. God did not create the world by saying: Matter is evil and it must be avoided. No world would have come into being if the Gods had thought like this. The world could only emanate from the Divine because the Gods ordained that spirit should be directly and immediately active in matter.

If man realizes that his best life in every sphere is directed according to divine intention, he must choose a form of education that does not alienate him from the world, but makes him a being whose soul and spirit betake themselves into the body throughout his whole life. A man who must be continually casting off his body when he immerses himself in thought, is no true thinker.

. . . .

Thus, what we can do in a healthy way through the artistic, through developing the intellect out of artistic foundations, is related to the waking life, whereas all physical culture has a definite relation to the child's life of sleep. If we wish really to understand the form that healthy culture and exercise of the body should take, we must first ask this question: " How does bodily exercise affect the life of sleep ? "

All bodily activity arises, soul-spiritually, from the will—is indeed an out-streaming of will-impulses into the organism of movement. Even in purely mental activity the will is active and is flowing into the limbs. If we sit at a desk and think out decisions which are then carried out by others, our will-impulses are, nevertheless, streaming into our limbs. In this instance we simply hold them back, restrain them. We ourselves may sit still, but the orders we give are really an instreaming of the will into our own limbs. We must therefore first discover what is of importance in these physically active impulses of the will, if their unfolding is to have the right effect upon the state of sleep.

Now everything that is transformed into action by the human will sets up a certain organic process of combustion. When I think, I solidify my organism, I deposit solids within it. When I will, I burn up something in my organism—only this inner process of burning up must not be identified with external combustion, with the combustion of chemistry or physics. When a candle is alight there is an external process of combustion, but only materialistic thinking can compare the inner process of combustion with the burning of a lighted candle. In the human organization the processes of outer nature are taken hold of by forces of the soul and spirit so that within the human body, and even within the plant, the outer substances of nature are quite differently active. Similarly, the burning process within the human being is altogether different from the process of combustion we see in the lighted candle. Yet a certain kind of combustion is always induced in the body when we will, even though the impulse does not bring us into bodily movement.

Now because we generate this process of inner combustion, we bring about something in our organism that sleep alone can rectify. In a certain sense we should literally burn up our bodies if sleep did not perpetually reduce combustion to its right degree of intensity, reduce it in a fine and intimate way, and not in the crude sense of natural science. Sleep regulates the inner burning by spreading it over the whole organism, whereas otherwise it would confine itself to the organs of movement.

Now there are two ways of carrying out bodily movements. Think of the kind of exercises children are often given to do. The idea is—(everything is " idea " in a materialistic age, in spite of its belief that it is dealing with facts)—that the child ought to make this or that kind of movement, in its games or gymnastics, because only so will he grow up to be a civilized human being. As a rule, movements to which grown-up people are also accustomed are considered the best, and since the ideal is that the child should grow up an exact copy of his elders, he is made to do the same kind of gymnastics. That is to say, a certain opinion is held about what is proper to the right sort of man, and this must apply also to the child.

Thus out of an idea, out of the abstract, although it is a question of the actual and material, something material is forced on to the child. Gymnastic apparatus is so contrived as to oblige the child to make the desired movements. But this sets up processes of combustion which the human organism is no longer capable of adjusting. Restless sleep is the result of such merely external methods of physical culture.

Once again, these things are not so crude as to be confirmed by orthodox Medicine, but they take place nevertheless in the finer and more delicate processes of the human body. If we give children only these conventional gymnastic exercises, they cannot get the deep, sound sleep they need, and the bodily constitution cannot be sufficiently refreshed and restored in sleep.

If we educate the child artistically, if we bring everything in the school to the child in an artistic way, then just as the over-richness of the artistic life produces a longing for the impoverishment implicit in intellectual work—the intellectual is then drawn elementally out of the artistic—so there also arises in the child who is artistically engaged a certain hunger for bodily activity, and this is so because artistic work brings the whole man into action. Nothing so easily induces a craving for bodily exercise as artistic activity. If the child has been occupied artistically for about two hours—and the length of time must be carefully arranged—something that longs for expression in quite definite movements of the body begins to stir in the organism. Art creates a real hunger for right movements of the body.

Thus what has been done with the hands in painting and drawing, or with the voice in singing, or—which should be begun as soon as possible—with a musical instrument, what has been done, therefore directly through or with the body, we gradually lead over, we let stream out into games, into spatial movement in play. We must thus have a continuation of what goes on within the organism in the children's artistic work. Physical training is then drawn forth from the other work at school, and there is an intimate connection between the two.

If the child is only given such physical exercises as his artistic work makes him desire, he will get the kind of sleep he needs. If help can be given for a right waking life by drawing the intellectual out of the artistic, a right sleeping life, in which all the processes of combustion are harmonized in the organism, can be cultivated by developing bodily training also from out of the artistic element. As far as the body is concerned, nothing is more essential than that the teacher himself should be an artist through and through. The more joy the teacher can experience in beautiful forms, in music, the more he longs to pass from abstract words into the rhythms of poetry; the more of the plastic-musical there is in him, the better will he be able to arrange such games and exercises as offer the child an opportunity for artistic expression. But alas! our civilization to-day would like the spirit to be easy of access, and people do not feel inclined to strive too strenuously for spiritual ideals.

As I said in a previous lecture, most people—while admitting the inadequacy of their own education—claim at the same time to know what education ought to be, and are quite ready to lay down the law about it. There is thus no great inclination to consider these fine processes in the human organism, to ask how gymnastics can proceed artistically out of artistic activity, and what the human organism calls for as outer movement in space. Little enough artistic feeling is brought to bear on the solution of these problems. The reading of books is the main occupation of the modern intellectual; people study Greek ideals, and a revival of the " Olympic Games " has become a catch phrase, though this revival is of a purely external nature. The Olympic Games are never studied from the point of view of the needs of the human organism, as they were in Greece, for modern study is all book-learning, based on documents or outer traditions that have been handed down.

Now modern men are not ancient Greeks, and they do not understand the part played by the true Olympic Games in the culture of Greece. In those days the children were taught dancing, wrestling, and the like by the gymnasts, as I have described. But where did the Greeks learn this? They learnt it precisely from the Olympic Games, which were not only artistic but religious in their nature—a true offspring of Greek culture. In their Olympic Games the Greeks lived wholly given up to an atmosphere of art and religion, and therefore with a true educational instinct they could bring these elements into the gymnastic exercises given to children.

Abstract, prosaic, inartistic forms of physical culture are contrary to all true education, because they are contrary to the real development of the human being. It would be far better to-day if, instead of trying to find out from books how to revive the Olympic Games, people made some attempt to understand the inner nature of man. For then they would realize that all physical education not based on the inner needs of the organism sets up an excessive process of combustion. The result of performing such exercises in childhood will lead, in later life, to flabbiness of the muscular system. The muscles will be incapable of following the soul and spirit.

A false intellectual education for our waking life inwardly hardens the body and causes us to carry our bones around like a burden and not to move them resiliently with the soul, and to this we add flaccid limbs too strongly subject to combustion. And so man has gradually become a sort of balloon bound to a log of wood, a creature held down by the weight of salts within him, yet, because of wrong combustion processes in him, wanting to escape, to fly away from it. An intimate knowledge of man is necessary before a true relationship can be established between these two processes of combustion and salt-formation. Then the hardening that arises when we lead over the artistic into the intellectual element we balance by the right kind of combustion, which so works into the life of sleep, that the child sleeps deeply and peacefully. The restlessness and fidgetiness caused by most modern systems of bodily training are then absent. Children who are forced to practise the wrong kind of physical exercises fidget in soul during sleep, and in the morning, when the soul returns to the body, restlessness and faulty processes of combustion have been set up in the organism.

Our conceptions must therefore be widened by knowledge, for all this will show you that a profound understanding of human nature is essential. If in this earthly existence we hold man to be the most precious creation of the gods, the great question must be: What have the gods placed before us in man? How can we best develop what in man has been entrusted to us here on earth?

. . . .

Up to the seventh year the child is through and through an imitative being, and from the time of the change of teeth onwards, his inner nature seeks beyond anything else to shape itself according to what is revealed to it by natural authority—in the widest sense of the word.

A long time ago now, I wrote *The Philosophy of Spiritual Activity*, and in view of what I said there, I do not think you will accuse me of laying undue stress upon any exclusive principle of authority in social life. Although what is revealed in human life is spiritually under the impulse of freedom, it is just as fully subject to law as the life of nature. It is, therefore, not for us to decide according to our likes or dislikes what kind of education should be given to our children between the time of the change of teeth and adolescence. Education should rather be dictated by the needs of human nature itself. Accordingly, up to the second dentition, at about the seventh year, the child imitates in every gesture, in every attitude, nay, even in the pulsations of the blood and in the rhythms of the breath and of the various vessels, everything that goes on around him; from birth to the age of seven, the environment is the model which the child copies. Similarly from the seventh to the fourteenth or fifteenth years, to the age of puberty, he must unfold a free spiritual activity under the influence of natural authority. This must be so if development is to be healthy and free, and if the child is rightly to use his freedom in later life.

The faculty of personal judgment is not ripe until the fourteenth or fifteenth year. Only then has the child developed to a point where the teacher is justified in appealing to his faculty of judgment. At the age of fourteen or fifteen he can reason things out for himself, but before this age we injure him, we retard his development if we continually enter into "whys and wherefores". The whole of later life is immeasurably benefited if, between the seventh and fourteenth years (approximately, of course), we have been able to accept a truth not because we see its underlying reason—indeed, our intellect is not mature enough for this—but because we feel that the teacher whom we revere and love holds it to be true. Our sense of beauty grows in the right way if we are able to accept the teacher's standard of the beautiful—the teacher to whom we give a spontaneous, and not a forced respect.

We shall rightly experience the good, so that we tread its path in later life, if we are not given a code of behaviour to follow, but have realized from the teacher's own warmhearted words how much he loves a good deed and hates a bad one. His words can make us so warmly responsive to the good and so coldly averse to evil, that we turn naturally to the good because the teacher himself loves it. Then we grow up, not bound hand and foot by dogma, but filled with a spontaneous love for what is true, beautiful and good to the beloved teacher. If during the first period of school life we have learnt to adopt his standard of truth, beauty and goodness, a standard he has been able to express in artistic imagery, the impulse for these virtues becomes a second nature, for it is not the intellect that develops goodness. A man who has over and over again been told dogmatically to do this, or not to do that, has a cold, matter-of-fact feeling for the good, whereas one who has learnt in childhood to feel sympathy with goodness and antipathy to evil, who out of his feeling has preserved his enthusiasm for the good and his power to shun evil, has drawn right into his whole rhythmic organism the capacity to respond to the good and to be repelled by what is evil. In later life it is as though, under the influence of evil, he practically could not breathe, as if by evil the breathing and the rhythmic system were adversely affected.

It is really possible to achieve this, if, after the child has reached his seventh year, we allow the principle of natural authority to supersede that of imitation, which, as we have seen, must be predominant in the earlier years. Naturally, authority must not be enforced, for this is just the error of those methods of education that attempt to enforce authority by corporal punishment.

I have heard that what I said yesterday in this connection seemed to suggest that this form of punishment had already been entirely superseded. As a matter of fact, what I said was that the humanitarian feelings of to-day would like to do away with it. I was told that the custom of caning in England is still very general, and that my words had created a wrong impression. I am sorry that this should have been so, but the point I want to make is that in true education authority must never be maintained by force, and above all not by the cane. It must arise naturally from what we ourselves are. In body, soul, and spirit we are true teachers if our observation of human nature has brought us a true understanding of man. True observation of man sees in the growing human being a work of divine creation. There is no more wonderful spectacle in the whole world than to see in the child how, from birth on, the definite gradually emerges from the indefinite in the body, how indefinite movements, irrelevant, arbitrary movements change into such as are determined by the soul, how more and more the inner being expresses itself outwardly, and the spiritual element in the body comes gradually to the surface. This being which the divine world has sent down to earth, and which we feel is revealing itself in the body, becomes a revelation of the Divine itself. The growing human being is indeed its most splendid manifestation. If we learn to know this growing human being—not from the point of view of ordinary anatomy and physiology, but with understanding of how the soul and spirit stream down into the body—then all our knowledge of man changes into religion, into truly pious and humble reverence in face of what streams into the surface of things from out of divine depths. Then, as teachers, we have a certain quality that bears and sustains us, and that becomes for the child a natural authority in which he places spontaneous trust. Instead of arming ourselves with the cane—or using any form of inner punishment such as I mentioned yesterday—we should arm ourselves with a true knowledge of man, with the faculty of true observation. This will grow into an inner moral-religious sense, into a moral-religious reverence for God's creation. We then have a true position in the school and we realize how absolutely essential it is in all education to watch for those moments when the child's whole nature undergoes a mighty change, a metamorphosis.

Such a metamorphosis occurs, for instance, between the ninth and tenth year, though with one child it may be earlier, with another later. As a rule it occurs between the ages of nine and ten. Many things in life are passed by unobserved by the materialist. True observation of the human being tells us that something very remarkable happens between the ninth and tenth year. Outwardly, the child becomes restless; he cannot come to terms with the outer world and seems to draw back from it with a certain timidity. In a subtle way this happens to almost every child—indeed, if it does not occur, the child is abnormal. We must observe this, for in the child's life of feeling a great question arises between the ninth and tenth year; he cannot formulate this question mentally, nor can he express it in words. It is all feeling, and so is all the more strongly present and calls all the more intensely for recognition. What does the child seek at this age?

Till now, reverence for the teacher has been a natural impulse within him, but at this age he wants the teacher to prove himself worthy of this reverence in some special way. Uncertainty rises in the child, and when we observe this we must do something about it in response. There is no need at all to think anything out; we may be specially loving in our dealings with the child, specially aware of him and encouraging in what we say. Whatever it is we do, through our special attitude and through the child noticing that the teacher has him specially at heart and enters into his situation, we save him at this time from a precipice. This is of far-reaching significance, for if this sense of insecurity remains it will continue through the whole of later life, unnoticed by the one concerned, but none the less expressed in the character, temperament, and bodily health.

We must understand how everywhere the spirit works in matter and hence upon the health of the body, and how the spirit must be nurtured that it may rightly affect the health. A true art of education emphatically shows us that we must see spirit and matter to be in harmony and never in opposition. We must recognise what we owe to education in our modern civilisation which has separated everything. To-day we have a materialism; in this we live when we think about nature, and when people are dissatisfied with the results of this conception of nature, they think out a spiritualism, trying to reach the spirit through all sorts of things which really contradict science.

This is one of the tragedies of our day. A materialism which intellectualizes everything is now only able to understand the concepts it has itself evolved about matter; materialism, however, can never reach the heart of matter. And modern spiritualism? Its adherents want the spirits to be tangible, to reveal themselves materially by means of table-turning, physical phenomena and so on. They must not be allowed to remain spiritual, and thus invisible and intangible, because men are too lazy to penetrate to where they are.

Through these things man has fallen into a strangely tragic position. Materialism speaks only of matter—never of the spirit. But in reality materialism does not even understand matter, but speaks of it only in highly distilled abstractions, while spiritualism, imagining that it is speaking of the spirit, is concerned only with matter.

Our civilization is thus divided into materialism and spiritualism—a strange phenomenon indeed! For materialism understands nothing of matter, and spiritualism nothing of spirit.

And so we have the remarkable fact that the whole man has fallen into body and spirit. True education, however, must bring about a harmony between the two. It can never be too strongly emphasized that the goal of education must be for man once more to understand something of the spirit in matter, to grasp the material world with understanding from out of the spiritual. We find the spirit if we understand how to take hold of the material world rightly, and if we understand something of the spirit we find, not a materialized spirituality but a real and actual spiritual world.

If we are to educate humanity rightly, upwards and not downwards, we need the reality of the world of spirit and an intelligent comprehension of the world of matter.

VIII

READING, WRITING AND NATURE STUDY

In the previous lectures I have shown that when the child reaches the usual school age—at the transitional time of the change of teeth—all teaching should be given in an artistic, pictorial form. To-day, I propose to carry further the ideas already put before you and to show how this method appeals directly to the child's life of heart and feeling, and out of this life develops everything.

Let us take a few characteristic examples to show how writing can be derived from the artistic element of painting and drawing. I have already said that if a system of education is to harmonize with the natural development of the human organism, the child must be taught to write before he learns to read. The reason for this is that in writing the whole being is more active than is the case in reading. Writing entails the movement of only one particular member, but fundamentally speaking, the forces of the whole being must lend themselves to this movement. In reading, only the head and the intellect are engaged, and in a truly organic system of education we must develop everything out of the qualities and forces of the child's whole nature.

We will assume that we have been able to give the child some idea of flowing water; he has learnt to form a mental picture of waves and flowing water. We now proceed to make the child attentive to the initial sound, the initial letter

of the word "wave". Thus we turn our attention to the initial letter of characteristic words as we speak them out. We indicate that the surface of water rising into waves follows this line.

And from making the movement of this line, we bring the child to drawing it, and so to making the W. The child is thus introduced to the form of the letter "W" in writing. The W has arisen from the picture of a wave. In the first place the child is given a mental picture, or pictures which can lead over to the letters which he then learns to write. We may let the child draw the form of the mouth:

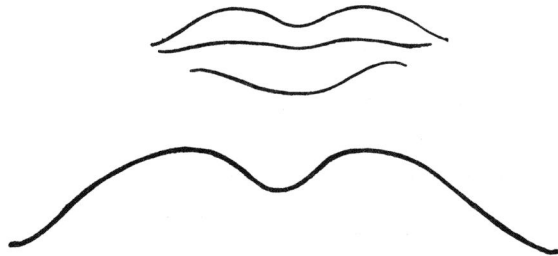

and then we introduce to him the first letter of the word "mouth". In one of our evening talks* I gave you another example. The child draws the form of a fish; when the fundamental form is firmly in his mind, we pass on to the initial letter of the word "fish".

* (Between the lectures there were meetings for discussion and questions, at which Rudolf Steiner often spoke.)

A great many letters can be treated in this way; others will have to be derived somewhat differently. Suppose, for instance, we give the child an imaginative idea of the movement of the sounding wind. This is the better way with little children, though, of course, there are many possibilities. We describe the on-rushing wind and let the child imitate its sound and so come to such a form as this:

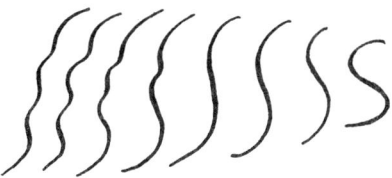

Thus by holding fast in painting the form of definitely shaped objects, movements or even activities, we can develop nearly all the consonants.

In the case of the vowels we must rather turn to gesture, for the vowels are an expression of man's inner being. "A" (ah), for example, inevitably contains an element of wonder, of astonishment. Eurhythmy will prove to be of great assistance here, for there we have gestures that truly correspond to feeling. The "I", the "A" and all the other vowels can be drawn from the corresponding gesture in eurhythmy, for the vowels must be derived from movements that accompany the feelings out of the life of the human being.

In this way we can proceed to the abstract nature of writing from the entirely concrete elements of painting-drawing, drawing-painting. We then succeed in making the child start from feeling called up by a picture; he then becomes able to relate to the actual letters the quality of soul contained in the feeling. The principle underlying writing thus arises from the feeling life of the soul.

When we come to reading, our efforts must simply be in the direction of getting the child to recognize—and this time in his head—of what has already been elaborated through the bodily forces as a whole. Reading is then recognized as an activity in which he has already been employed. This is of the very greatest significance. The whole process of development is spoilt if the child is led straight away to what is abstract, if he is taught to carry out any activity by means of a purely mental concept. On the other hand, a healthy growth will always ensue if the actual activity is introduced first, and the idea is only afterwards unfolded out of the activity. Reading is essentially a mental act. Therefore, if reading is taught first, and not after writing, the child is prematurely involved in a process of development exclusively concerned with the head instead of with the forces of his whole being.

By such methods as these, education can be guided into a sphere that embraces the whole man—into the realm of art. This must indeed be the aim of all our teaching up to the age of about nine and a half. Pictures, rhythms, measure—these qualities must pervade all our teaching. Everything else is premature.

It is for this reason utterly impossible before this age to convey anything to the child in which strong distinctions are made between himself and the outer world. The child only begins to realize himself as a being apart from the outer world between the ninth and tenth year. Hence, when he first comes to school, we must make all outer things appear as living beings. We shall not merely speak of the plants, but we shall speak of them as living beings, as holding converse with us and with each other in such a way that the child's outlook on nature and man is filled with imagination. The plants, the trees, the clouds all speak to him, and at this age he must really feel no separation between himself and the outer world. We must give him the feeling in an artistic way that just as he himself can speak, so everything that surrounds him also speaks.

The more we enable the child thus to flow out into his whole environment, the more vividly we describe plant, animal and stone, so that in them weaving, articulate spirituality is wafted towards him, the more adequately do we respond to the demands of his innermost being in these early years. They are years when the feeling life of the soul must flow into the processes of breathing and of the circulation of the blood and into the whole vascular system—indeed into the whole human organism. If we educate in this sense, the child's life of feeling will be called on in a way right for our times, so that the child will develop strongly and naturally in its organism and life of soul.

It is of incalculable benefit to the child if we develop this element of feeling in writing and then allow a faint echo of the intellect to enter as he re-discovers in reading what he has already experienced in writing. There is then a gentle accompaniment from the intellect. This is the very best way of leading the child on towards his ninth year.

Between the ages of seven and nine or nine-and-a-half it is essential that the teaching shall make a direct appeal to the element of feeling. The child must receive the various forms of the letters into his life of feeling. This is very important. We harden the child's nature unduly, we over-strengthen the forces of bone and cartilage and sinew in relation to the rest of the organism, if we teach him to write mechanically, making him trace arbitrary curves and lines for the letters, making use only of his bodily mechanism without calling upon the eye as well.

If we also call upon the eye—and the eye is of course connected with the movements of the hand—by developing the letters in an artistic way, so that the letter does not spring from merely mechanical movements of the hand, the eye itself will take pleasure in the results of its own activity. Qualities of the soul are thus brought rightly into play, and the life of feeling develops at an age when it can best flow into the physical organism with healing power.

· · · · · · · ·

I wonder what you would say if you were to see someone with a plate of fish in front of him, carefully cutting away the flesh and consuming the bones! You would certainly be afraid the bones might choke him and that in any case he would not be able to digest them. On another level—the level of the soul—exactly the same thing happens when we give the child dry, abstract, prosaic ideas instead of living pictures, instead of something that engages the activities of his whole being. These dry, abstract, prosaic concepts must only be there as a kind of support for the pictures that are to arise in the soul.

When we make use of this imaginative, pictorial method in education in the way I have described, we so orientate the child's nature that his concepts will always be mobile. We shall find that when he has passed the age of nine or nine-and-a-half, we can lead him on in a beautifully organic way to an understanding of an outer world in which he must, of necessity, learn to distinguish himself from his environment.

When we have given sufficient time to speaking of the plants as articulate beings, allowing the child as he looks at the plant world to experience it in living pictures, we can then introduce something he can learn in the best possible way from the plants if we begin to speak of it between the ninth and tenth year, gradually carrying it further during the tenth and eleventh.

The human organism is now at this stage ready to relate itself inwardly to the plant-world by way of ideas. But naturally, in an education aiming at the living development of the human being, the way we speak of the plants must be very different from such methods as are used for no other reason than that they were usual in our own school days. To give the child a plant or flower and then make him learn its name, the number of its stamens, the petals and so forth, has absolutely no meaning for human life, or at most only a conventional one.

Whatever is taught the child in this way remains quite foreign to him. He is merely aware of being forced to learn it, and those who teach botany to a child in his tenth or eleventh year in this form, know nothing of the real connections of nature. To study some plant by itself, preserve it in a herbarium and then lay it out on a table for study, is just as though we were to pull out a single hair and observe it as it lay there before us. The hair by itself is nothing; it cannot grow of itself and has no meaning apart from the human head. Its meaning lies simply and solely in the fact that it grows on the head of a man, or the skin of an animal. Only in its connections has it any living import. Similarly, the plant only has living significance in its relation to the earth, to the forces of the sun and, as I shall presently show, to other forces also. In teaching children about a plant therefore, we must never consider it except in its relationship to the earth and to the sun.

I can only make a very rough sketch here of something that can be illustrated in pictures in a number of lessons. Here (drawing on the blackboard) is the earth; the roots of the plant are intimately bound up with the earth, and belong to it. Never must any other thought be awakened in the child than that the earth and the root belong to one another. And again, no other thought must be awakened than that the blossom is drawn forth from the plant by the rays of the sun. The child is thus led out into the cosmos in a living way.

The teacher who has sufficient inner vitality, can best tell the child at this particular age of how the plant is placed livingly into its cosmic existence. To begin with, we can awaken a feeling of how the earth-substances permeate the root, the root then struggles to free itself from the earth and sends a shoot upwards; this shoot is born of the earth, and unfolds into leaf and flower by the light and warmth of the sun. The sun draws out the blossoms and the earth retains the root.

Then we call the child's attention—again in a living way— to the fact that a moist earth, earth inwardly watery in nature, works quite differently upon the root than does a dry earth; that the roots become shrivelled up in a dry soil and are living and filled with sap in a moist, watery earth.

Again, we explain how the rays of the sun, falling perpendicularly to the earth, call forth flowers of plants like yellow dandelions, buttercups and roses. When the rays of the sun fall obliquely, however, as if stroking across the plant, we have plants like the mauve autumn crocus, and so on. Everywhere we can point to living connections between root and earth, between blossom and sun.

Having thus placed the child's idea-picture livingly into

the cosmos we pass on to describe how the whole of its growth is finally concentrated in the seed vessels from which the new plant is to grow. Then one day, to anticipate the future a little—in a form suited to the age of the child—we must begin to disclose a truth of which it is difficult, as yet, to speak openly, because modern science regards it as pure superstition, or so much fantastic mysticism.

Nevertheless it is indeed a fact that just as the sun draws the coloured blossom out of the plant, so is it the forces of the moon which develop the again contracting seed-vessels. Seed-vessels are brought forth by the forces of the moon. In this way we place the plant as a living thing into the working of the sun, moon and earth. True, one cannot enter yet into this working of the moon forces, for if the children were to say at home that they had been taught about the connection between seed-vessels and the moon, their parents might easily be prevailed upon by scientific friends to remove them from such a school—even if the parents themselves were willing to accept such things! We shall have to be somewhat reticent on this subject and on many others too, in these materialistic days.

By this radical example I wished, however, to show you how necessary it is to develop living ideas—ideas that are drawn from actual reality and not from something that has no existence in itself. For in itself—without the sun and the earth—the plant has no existence.

We must now show the child something further. Here (drawing on the blackboard) is the earth; it grows out a little, it produces a hill; but the hill is penetrated by the forces of air and sun. It remains earth substance no longer; it changes into something that lies between the sappy leaf and the root in the dry earth—into the trunk of a tree. On this plant that has grown out of the earth, other plants grow—the branches. The child thus realizes that the trunk of the tree is really the earth which has sprouted upwards. This also gives an idea of the inner kinship between the earthly and all that finally becomes woody. In order to bring this fully home to the child, we show him how the wood decays, becoming more and more earthly till it finally falls into dust, and so becomes altogether similar to the earth. Then we can explain how sand and stone have their origin in what was once really destined to become plant, how the earth is like one huge plant, a giant tree out of which the various plants grow like branches.

Here we develop an idea intelligible to the child; the whole earth is a living being of which the plants are an integral part.

It is all-important that the child should not get into his head the distorted ideas suggested by modern geology—that the earth consists merely of mineral substances and mineral forces. For the plant growth-forces belong to the earth as much as the mineral forces. And now another point of great significance.—To begin with, we avoid speaking of the mineral as such. The child is curious about many things, but we shall find that he is no longer anxious to know what the stones are, if we have conveyed to him a living idea of the plants as an integral part of the earth and drawn forth from the earth by the sun.

The child has no real interest in the mineral as such. And it is very much to the good if up to the eleventh or twelfth year he is not interested in the dead mineral substances, but can think of the earth as a living being, as a tree that has already crumbled to dust, from which all the plants grow like branches.

From this point of view it is easy to pass on to the different plants. For instance, I say to the child: The root of such and such a plant is trying to find soil—its blossoms, remember, are drawn forth by the sun. Suppose that the roots cannot find any soil but only decaying earth—then the result will be that the sun does not trouble itself to draw out the blossoms. Then we have a plant which fails to find the earth properly, and so has no real roots, but also no real flower—a fungus, or mushroom-like growth. We now explain how a plant like a fungus, having found no proper soil in the earth, is able to take root where the earth has already become a little plant-like, in the plant-hill of the tree-trunk. The greyish-green lichen appears on the tree—it is a parasitic plant.

In this way the possibility becomes ours to draw from out of the living, weaving forces of the earth herself, that which expresses itself in the different plants. And when the child has been given living ideas of the growth of the plants, we can pass on from this study of the living plant to a survey of the face of the earth.

In some regions yellow flowers abound; in others the plants are stunted in their growth, and in each case the face of the earth is different. Thus we reach geography, which can play an extraordinarily important part in the child's development if we lead up to it from the plants.

We should try to give an idea of the face of the earth by connecting the forces at work on its surface with the varied plant-life we find in the different regions. Then we unfold a living instead of a dead intellectual faculty in the child. The very best age for this is the time between the ninth, tenth, eleventh, and the twelfth year. If we can give the child this conception of the weaving activity of the earth whose inner vital force brings forth the different forms of the plants, we give him living and not dead ideas. Ideas must develop just as a limb of the body. A limb has to develop in earliest youth. If we enclosed a hand for instance, in an iron glove, it could not grow. Yet it is constantly being said that the ideas we give to children should be as definite as possible—they should be definitions and the children ought always to be forming them. But nothing is more hurtful to the child than definitions and sharply contoured ideas, for these have no quality of growth. Now the human being must grow as his organism grows. The child must be given mobile concepts—concepts whose form is constantly changing as he becomes more mature. If we have a certain idea when we are forty years of age, it should not be a mere repetition of something we learnt when we were ten. It ought to have changed its form, just as our limbs and the whole of our organism have changed.

Living ideas cannot be roused if we only give the child what is nowadays called "science"—the dead knowledge which we so often find teaches us nothing! Rather must we give the child an idea of what is living in nature. Then its soul will develop in a body which grows as nature herself. We shall not then do, as is so often done in education: implant in a body engaged in a process of natural development, elements of soul-life that are dead and incapable of growth. We shall foster a living, growing soul in a living, growing physical organism—and this alone serves a true development.

This true development can best be induced by studying the life of plants in intimate connection with the configuration of the earth. The child should feel the life of the earth and the life of the plants as a unity: knowledge of the earth should be at the same time a knowledge of the world of the plants.

The child should first of all be shown how the lifeless mineral is a residue of life, for the tree decays and falls into dust. At the particular age of which I am now speaking, nothing in the way of mineralogy should be taught the child. He must first be given ideas and concepts of what is living. That is the essential thing.

. . . .

Just as the world of the plants should be related to the earth and the child should learn to think of them as the offspring, the last, outward-growing product of a living earth-organism, so should the animal-world as a whole be related to man. The child is thus enabled—in a living way—to find his own place in nature and in the world. He begins to understand that the plant-world belongs to the earth. On the other hand, however, we teach him to realize that the various animal-species spread over the world represent, in a certain sense, the path towards human development. The plants have kinship to the earth, the animals to man—this should be the basis from which we start. I can only justify it here as a principle; the actual details of what is taught to a child of ten, eleven or twelve years concerning the animal world, must be worked out with true artistic feeling.

In a very simple, even primitive way, we begin by calling the child's attention to the nature of man. This is quite possible if the preliminary artistic foundations have already been laid. The child will learn to understand, in however simple a sense, that man has a threefold organization. First, there is the head. A hard shell encloses the system of nerves and the softer parts that lie within it. The head may thus be compared with the round earth within the cosmos. We shall do our utmost to give the child a concrete, artistic understanding of the head-system and then lead on to the second member—the rhythmic system which includes the organs of breathing and circulation of the blood. Having spoken of the artistic modelling of the cup-like formation of the skull which encloses the soft parts of the brain, we pass on to consider the series of bones in the spinal column and the branching ribs. We shall study the characteristics of the chest, with its breathing and circulatory systems. Then we reach the third member—the system of metabolism and limbs. As organs of movement, the limbs really maintain and support the metabolism of the body, for the processes of combustion are regulated by their activities. The limbs are connected with metabolism. Limbs and metabolism must be taken together; they constitute the third member of man's being.

To begin with, then, we make this threefold division of man. If our teaching is pervaded with the necessary artistic feeling and is given in the form of pictures, it is quite possible to convey to the child this conception of man as a threefold being.

We now draw the child's attention to the different animal species spread over the earth. We begin with the lowest forms of animal life, with creatures whose softer organic parts lie inside and are surrounded by shell-like formations. Certain members of the lower animal species consist, strictly speaking, merely of a sheath surrounding the protoplasm. We show the child how the form of the human head appears —primitively of course—in these lower creatures.

Our head is a lower animal, fashioned to the highest degree of development. The head, and more particularly the nervous system, must not be correlated with the mammals or the apes, but with the lowest forms of animal life. We must also go far, far back in the earth's history, to the most ancient formations and there we find animals consisting wholly of a kind of elementary head. Thus we try to make the lower animal world intelligible to the child as a primitive head-organization.

We then take the animals somewhat higher in the scale—the fishes and their allied species. Here the spinal column is especially developed and we explain that these "half-way" animals are beings in whom the human rhythmic system has developed—the other members being stunted. In the lowest animals, then, we find at an elementary stage, the organization corresponding to the human head. In the animal species grouped round the fishes, we find a one-sided development of the human chest-organization. Then finally the system comprising the limbs and metabolism brings us to the higher animals.

The organs of movement are developed in great diversity of form, especially in the higher animals. The mechanism of a horse's foot, a lion's pad, or the feet of the wading animals—all these give us a golden opportunity for artistic description. Or again, we can compare the limbs of man with the one-sided development we find in the limbs of the apes. In short, we begin to understand the higher animals by studying the plastic structure of the organs of movement, or the digestive organs.

Beasts of prey differ from the ruminants in that the latter have very long intestinal track, whereas in the former, while the intestinal coil is short, the system connecting the heart and blood circulation with the digestive processes is strongly and powerfully developed. A study of the organization of the higher animals shows at once how one-sided is its development in comparison with the system of limbs and metabolism in man. We can give a concrete picture of how the frontal part of the spine in the animal is really nothing but head. The whole digestive system is continued right on into the head. The animal's head essentially belongs to the digestive organs —to the stomach and intestines. In man, on the other hand, that which has remained, as it were, in the virginal state—the soft parts of the brain with their enclosing, protecting shell of bone—is placed above the limb and metabolic system.

The head organization in man is thus raised a stage higher than in the animal, in which, as we have seen, it is merely a continuation of the metabolism. Yet man, as far as his head organization is concerned, goes back to what, in the simplest way, that organism provides—namely, soft substance within, surrounded by a cup-like bony formation.

It can be shown, in addition, how the jaws of certain animals can best be studied, when they are regarded as the frontmost limbs of the animal. In this way we best obtain a plastic understanding of the animal-head. Thus the human being emerges as a synthesis of three systems—head system, chest system, system of limbs and metabolism. In the animal world there is a one-sided development of the one or other system. Thus we have first, the lower animals—the crustaceans, for example, but also others, then the mammals, birds and so on, and then the chest-animals, which have chiefly developed the chest-system: the fishes, and creatures like them, the reptiles etc. We see, as it were, the animal

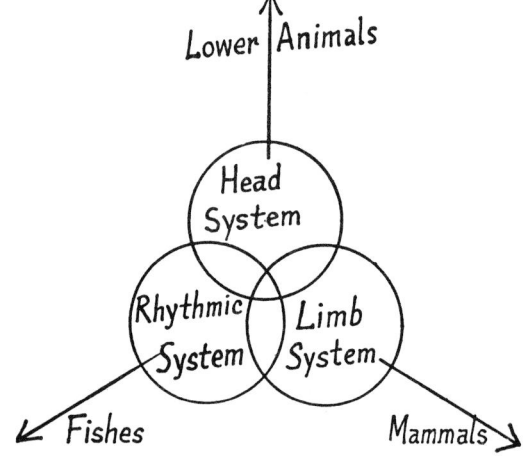

kingdom as a human being dismembered, spread out fan-like over the earth. We relate the world of the plants to the earth, and the diverse animal species to man who is, in fact, the synthesis of the entire animal world. Taking our start from man's physical organization, we give the child, in a simple way, an idea of the threefold nature of his being. Passing to the animals, we explain how in the different species there is always a one-sided development of certain organs, whereas in man these organs are united into one harmonious whole. This one-sided, specialized development is manifested by the chest organs in certain animals; in others by the lower intestines, and in others again, by the upper organs of digestion. In many forms of animal life—birds, for instance—we find metamorphoses of certain organs; the organs of digestion become the crop—and so forth.

We can characterize each animal species as representing a one-sided development of an organic system in man, so that the whole animal world appears as the being of man spread fan-wise over the earth in diversity of forms, man himself as being the synthesis of the whole animal kingdom.

When this has been made clear to the child so that he understands the animal world as the man who has developed his single organic systems onesidedly—the one system living on as this animal species; the other as that animal species—we can then ascend again to man. This should be when the child is approaching his twelfth year, for he can then understand as a matter of course that because man bears his spirit within him, he is a symptomatic unity, an artistic synthesis of the separate parts of his being, which are mirrored in the various species of animals. Only because man bears his spirit within him can he thus harmonize the lower animal organization into a whole. In a complicated way he transforms this into the head organization, correspondingly fitted into that of the breast, which he also develops so as to harmonize with the rest. He thus bears in himself what is in the fish organization, as also what is in the higher animal organization, but harmoniously arranged into a whole. The separate fragments of man, scattered over the world in the realm of the animals, are in man gathered together by the spirit into total being. Thus we relate man with the animal world, but man is at the same time raised above the animals because he is the bearer of the spirit.

The results of this kind of teaching will be perfectly

apparent to unprejudiced observation. Botany and knowledge of the plants, taught in the way I have indicated, work on the living world of ideas, and through his good sense place the human being rightly in the world, able to do his work, so that with his ideas he finds his way livingly through life. On the other hand, an equally living conception of his own relationship to the whole animal world specially strengthens the will.

You will naturally realize that what I have had to discuss here in some twenty minutes or so, must be developed stage by stage for a long period of time; we must gradually accustom the child to unite these ideas with his entire nature. Then they will enter into the part a man plays in the world by virtue of his strength of will. The will grows inwardly strong if a man in his own knowledge realizes that by grace of the living spirit, he himself develops as the synthesis of the animal kingdom. This goes into the will, into the forming of the will.

And so the aim of our educational work is not merely to teach facts about the plants and animals, but also to develop character—in short, the whole nature of the human being. We work for a right cultivation of the intelligence by our teaching about the plants, and of the will by our teaching about the animals. In this way we so relate the child between the ninth and twelfth year to these other creatures of the earth that, through a right intelligence and a due, self-confidence bestowing strength of will, he may find his way properly through the world.

And this above all is what we must achieve in education, that the human being so develops in regard to both these things. Out of feeling which we have cultivated in the child between seven and nine-and-a-half, we have developed intelligence and strength of will. Thinking, feeling and willing are then brought into a right relationship instead of developing as so often in a quite inorganic way. Everything is rooted in feeling. We must begin with the child's feeling life and from feeling in connection with the world, develop thinking through a comprehension of the kingdom of the plants. For the life of the plants will never admit of dead conceptions. Out of feeling also we develop the will if we lead the child to what rightly connects him with the animals, but also raises him above them.

Thus we strive to impart a right intelligence and a strong will to the human being. This indeed is our task in education, for this alone will make him fully man—and the evolution of full manhood is the goal of all education.

IX

Arithmetic, Geometry, History

Arithmetic and geometry—indeed all mathematics—occupy a unique position in education. Education can only be filled with the necessary vitality and give rise to a real interplay between the soul of the teacher and the soul of the child, if the teacher fully realizes the consequences of his actions and methods. He must know exactly what effect is made on the child by the treatment he receives in school, or anywhere else.

Now man is a being of body, soul and spirit, and his bodily nature is formed and moulded by the spirit. The teacher, then, must always be aware of what is taking place in the soul and spirit when any change occurs in the body, and again, what effect is produced in the body when influences are brought to bear on the life of spirit or soul.

Anything that works upon the child's life of mental picturing or representation—anything that is to say, of the nature of painting or drawing which are then led over into writing, or again, botany taught in the way indicated yesterday—all this has a definite effect. And here, above all, we must consider a higher member of man's being—a member to which I have already referred as the etheric body, or body of formative forces. The human being has, in the first place, his physical body. It is revealed to ordinary, physical sense-perception. Besides this physical body, however, he has an inner organization, perceptible only to Imaginative Cognition—a supersensible, etheric body. Again he has an organization perceptible only to Inspiration—the next stage of supersensible knowledge. (These expressions need not confuse us; they are merely terms.) Inspiration gives insight into the so-called astral body and into the real ego, the self of the human being.

Now from birth till death, this etheric body, this body of formative forces which is the first supersensible member of man's being, never separates from the physical body; that only happens at death. During sleep, the etheric organization remains with the physical body lying there in bed. When man sleeps, the astral body and ego-organization leave the physical and etheric bodies and enter them again at the moment of waking.

Now it is the physical and etheric bodies which are affected when the child is taught arithmetic or geometry, or when we lead him on to writing from the basis of drawing and painting. All this retains and continues to vibrate with the etheric body during sleep.—On the other hand, history or a study of the animal kingdom of which I spoke in yesterday's lecture, work only upon the astral body and ego-organization. What results from these studies we take out of the physical and etheric bodies into the spiritual world in sleep.

If, therefore, we are teaching the child plant-lore or writing, the effects are held back by the physical and etheric bodies during sleep, they continue to vibrate, whereas the results of history lessons or lessons on the nature of man are different, for they are carried out into the spiritual world by the ego and astral body. Thus there is a great difference in the effects produced by the different lessons.

We must realize that all impressions made on the child of an imaginative or pictorial nature have the tendency to become more and more perfect during sleep. On the other hand, everything we tell the child on the subject of history or the being of man, works on his organization of soul and spirit and tends to be forgotten, to become less perfect and grow dim during sleep. In the lessons, therefore, we have necessarily to consider whether the subject-matter will speak to the etheric and physical bodies or to the astral body and ego-organization.

Thus the study of the plant kingdom and the rudiments of writing and reading, of which I spoke yesterday, affect the physical and etheric bodies. All that is learnt of history—I shall speak about the teaching of this later on—or of man's relation to the animal kingdom affects the astral body and ego-organization—those higher members which pass out of the physical and etheric bodies during sleep. But the remarkable thing is that arithmetic and geometry affect both the physical-etheric and the astral and ego. Arithmetic and geometry are really like a chameleon; by their very nature they harmonize with every part of man's being. Whereas lessons on the plant and animal kingdoms should be given at a definite age, arithmetic and geometry must be taught through the whole period of childhood—though naturally in a form suited to the changing characteristics of the different life-periods.

It is all-important to remember that the body of formative forces (the etheric body) begins to function independently when it is abandoned by the ego and astral body. By virtue of its own inherent vibrational forces, it has ever the tendency to bring to perfection and elaborate what has been brought to it. As far as our astral body and ego are concerned, we are—stupid, shall I say? For instead of perfecting what has been conveyed to these members of our being, we make it less perfect. During sleep, however, our body of formative forces continues supersensibly to calculate, continues all that it has received as arithmetic and the like. We ourselves are then no longer within the physical and etheric bodies; but supersensibly, they continue to calculate or to draw geometrical figures and perfect them. If we are aware of this fact and plan our teaching accordingly, great vitality can be generated in the being of the child. We must, however, make it possible for the body of formative forces to perfect and elaborate what it has previously received.

In geometry, therefore, we must not take as our starting point the abstractions and intellectual constructions that are usually considered the right groundwork. We must begin with inner, not outer perception, by stimulating in the child a strong sense of symmetry, for instance.

Even in the case of the very youngest children we can begin

to do this. For example: we draw some figure on the blackboard, add a straight line, and indicate the beginning of the symmetrical line. Then we try to make the child realize that the figure is not complete and by every possible means to get the child to complete it out of himself. In this way we awaken an inner, active urge in the child to complete something as yet unfinished. This helps him to bring into action an absolutely right picture of something that is a reality. The teacher, of course, must have inventive talent, but that is always a very good thing. Above all else the teacher must have mobile, inventive thought. When he has given these exercises for a certain time, he will proceed to others. For instance, he may draw some such figure as this (left) on the

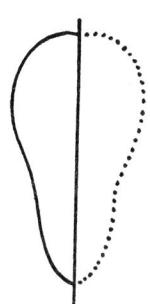

blackboard, and then he tries to awaken in the child an inner spatial impression of it. The outer line is then varied and the child gradually learns to draw an inner form corresponding to the outer (right). In the one the curves are absolutely straight-forward and simple. In the other, the lines curve outwards at various points. Then we should explain to the child that for the sake of inner symmetry he must make, in the inner figure, an inward curve at the place where the lines curve outwards in the outer figure. In the first diagram a simple line corresponds to another simple line, whereas in the second, an inward curve corresponds to an outward curve.

Or, again, we draw something of this kind, and then the

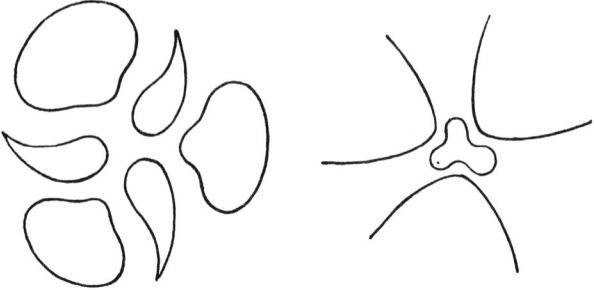

corresponding outer forms, so as to make an harmonious whole. We now seek the transition from this to another exercise in which we do not let the outer figures come together, but rather run away from each other into the undefined. Now the child gets the impression that this point wants to move off, that one has to go after it with these lines but cannot overtake it, it has flown away. Then the child realizes that the corresponding figure must be arranged correspondingly, so that, because this ran away, this must be specially bent inwards. I can only indicate the principles of the thing. Briefly, by working in this way, we give the child an idea of "a-symmetrical symmetries" and so prepare the body of formative forces in his waking life that during sleep it continues to vibrate, but in its vibrations perfects what has been absorbed during the day. Then the child will wake in an etheric body—and a physical body also—inwardly and organically stirred into activity. He will be full of life and vitality. This can, of course, only be achieved when the teacher has some knowledge of the working of the etheric body; if there is no such knowledge, all efforts in this direction will be mechanical and superficial.

A true teacher is not only concerned with the waking life but also with what takes place during sleep. In this connection it is important to understand certain things that happen to us all now and again. For instance, we may have pondered over some problem in the evening without finding a solution. In the morning we have solved the problem. Why?

Because the etheric body, the body of formative forces, has continued its independent activity during the night.

In many respects waking life is not a perfecting, but a disturbing process. It is necessary for us to leave our physical and etheric bodies to themselves for a time and not make them stupid by the activity of astral body and ego. This is proved by many things in life; for instance, by the example already given, of someone who is puzzling over a problem in the evening. When he wakes up in the morning he may feel slightly restless, but suddenly finds that the solution has come to him unconsciously during the night. These things are not fables; they actually happen and have been proved as conclusively as many another experiment. What has happened in this particular case? The work of the etheric body has continued through the night, and the human being has been asleep the whole time. That is not a normal occurrence, or a thing to be striven for. What is to be striven for, however, is to assist the continued activity of the etheric body during sleep, and we do this if, instead of beginning geometry with triangles and the like, where the intellectual element is already in evidence, we begin by conveying a concrete representation of space. In arithmetic, too, we must proceed in the same way. I will speak of this after the translation.

. . . .

A pamphlet on physics and mathematics written by Dr. von Baravalle (a teacher at the Waldorf School) will give you a splendid idea of how to bring concreteness into arithmetic and geometry. This whole mode of thought is extended in the pamphlet to the realm of physics as well, though it deals chiefly with higher mathematics. If we penetrate to its underlying spirit, it is a splendid guide for teaching mathematics in a way that corresponds to the organic needs of the child's being. A starting-point has indeed been created for a reform in the method of teaching mathematics and physics from earliest childhood up to the highest stages of instruction. We must, however, be able to extend to the domain of arithmetic, what is said about concrete conceptions of space in this pamphlet.

The whole point is that everything conveyed in an external way to the child by arithmetic or even by counting, destroys something in the human organism. To start from the unit and add to it piece by piece is simply to destroy the organism of man. But if we first awaken an awareness of the whole, then an awareness of the members of this whole—starting from the whole and then proceeding to its parts—the organism is made more alive. This must be borne in mind even when the child is learning to count. As a rule we learn to count by being made to observe purely external things—things of material, physical life.

First we have 1—we call this the unity. Then 2, 3, 4 and so forth, are added, unit by unit, and we have no idea whatever why the one follows the other, nor of what happens in the end. We are taught to count by being shown an arbitrary juxtaposition of units. I am well aware that there are many different methods for teaching children to count, but very little attention is paid nowadays to the principle of starting from the whole and then proceeding to the parts. It is the unit which the child, too, should first see as a whole. Everything is a unity, whatever it may be. Here we are obliged to illustrate it in a drawing. We must therefore draw a line; but we could use an apple just as well to do what I shall now do with a line:

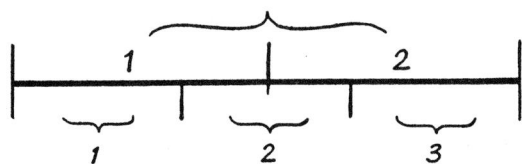

This, then, is 1. And now we go on from the whole to the parts, or members. Here, then, we have made of the 1, a 2, but the 1 still remains. The unit has been divided into two. Thus we arrive at the 2. And now we go on. By a further partition the 3 comes into being. Unity aways remains as the all-embracing whole. And so we go on through the 4, 5 and so on. Moreover, simultaneously and by some other means, we can give an idea of the extent to which it is possible to hold together in the mind the things that relate to number and we shall discover how really limited man is in his power of mental presentation where number is concerned.

In certain nations to-day the concept of number that is clearly held in the mind's eye only goes up to 10. Here in this country the money is reckoned up to 12. But that really represents the maximum of what is mentally visualized, for in reality we then begin over again and repeat the numbers. We first of all count up to 10, then we begin counting the tens, 2 times 10 = 20, 3 times 10 = 30. Here we are no longer considering the things themselves. We begin to calculate by using number itself, whereas the more elementary concept requires the things themselves to be clearly present in the mind.

To-day we are very proud of the fact that we are far advanced in our methods of counting compared with primitive peoples who depend on their ten fingers. But there is little foundation for this pride. We count up to 10 because we feel our members, the members of our hands. We feel our two hands symmetrically with their 10 fingers. This feeling also arises and is inwardly experienced by the child, and we must call forth the sense of number by a transition from the whole to the parts. Then we shall easily find the other transition which leads us to the counting in which one is added to another. Eventually, of course, we can pass on to the ordinary 1, 2, 3, etc. But this mere adding of one or more units must only be introduced as a second stage, for it only has a significance here in physical space. Whereas to divide a unity into its members has an inner meaning which can continue to vibrate in the etheric body, even when we are not there. It is important to know these things.

Having taught the child to count in this way, the following will also be important. We must not pass on to addition in a lifeless, mechanical way, merely adding one item to another in series. Life comes into the thing when we take our start, not from the parts of the addition but from the sum total itself. We take a number of objects, for example, we throw down a number of little balls. We have now got far enough in counting to be able to say: Here are 14 balls. Now we divide them, extending this concept of a part still further. Here we have 5, here 4, here 5 again. Thus we have separated the sum into 5 and 4 and 5. We pass from the sum to the items composing it, from the whole to the parts. The method we should use with the child is first to set down the sum before him and then let the child 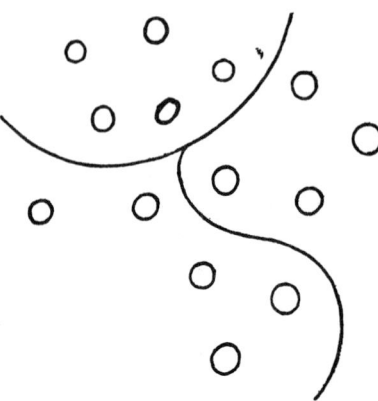 himself perceive how the given sum can be divided into several items.

This is exceedingly important. Just as to drive a horse we do not harness him tail foremost, so in the teaching of arithmetic we must have the right direction. We must start from a whole which is actually present in everything, from a reality, from what is present as a whole, and then pass on to the separate parts; later, we find our way back to the ordinary addition sum.

Continuing in this way, from the living whole to the separate parts, one touches the reality underlying all arithmetical calculations: i.e., the setting in vibration of the body of formative forces. This body needs a living stimulus for its formative, perfecting activity, which it will continue without any need of the presence of the astral body and ego-organization with their disturbing elements.

Your teaching work will also be essentially enhanced and vivified if you similarly reverse the other simple forms of calculation. To-day, one might say, they are standing on their heads and must be set upright. Try, for instance, to bring the child to say: "If I have 7, how much must I take away to get 3," instead of "What remains over if I take 4 from 7?" That we have 7 is the real thing, and what I have left is equally real; how much must we take away from 7 to get 3? Beginning with this form of thought we stand in the midst of life, whereas with the opposite form we are face to face with an abstraction. Proceeding in this way, we can easily revert to the other in due course. Thus, once more, in multiplication and division we should not ask what will result when we divide 10 into two parts, but how must we divide 10 to get the number 5. The real aspect is given; in life we want eventually to get at something which has real significance. Here are two children—10 apples are to be divided among them. Each of them is to get 5. These are the realities. What we have first to contribute is the abstract part that comes in the middle. Done in this way, things are always immediately adapted to life and should we succeed in this, the result will be that what is frequently the usual purely external way of adding, by counting up one thing after another with a deadening effect upon the arithmetic lessons, will become a vivifying force, of especial importance in this branch of our educational work. We must really take into account the sub-conscious part of man, that is to say, the part that not only works on in sleep but also works subconsciously in the waking hours. Man does not always think of everything. He is aware only of a small fragment of his soul's experience—nevertheless the rest is continuously active. Let us make it possible for the physical and etheric bodies of the child to work in a healthy way, realizing that we can only do so if we bring atmosphere, interest, life, especially into the lessons in arthmetic and geometry.

The question has arisen during this Conference as to whether it is really a good thing to continue the teaching of subjects for certain periods of time as we do in the Waldorf School. Now a right division of the lessons into periods is fruitful in the very highest degree. "Period" teaching means that one lesson shall not perpetually encroach upon another. Instead of having timetables setting forth definite hours—8 to 9, arithmetic, 9 to 10, history, religion, or whatever it may be—we give one main lesson on the same subject for two hours every morning for a period of three, four or five weeks. Then we pass on to another main lesson for perhaps five or six weeks, on a different subject, which if you like develops out of the previous work, but again is carried on during the two hours. The child thus concentrates upon a definite subject for some weeks.

The question was asked whether this would not result in the children forgetting too much of what they had been taught. If the lessons have been rightly taught, however, the previous subject will go on working in the subconscious regions while another is being taken. In "period" lessons we must always reckon with the subconscious processes in the child. There is nothing more fruitful than to allow the results of the teaching given during a period of three or four weeks to rest within the soul and so work on in the human being without interference. It will soon be apparent, when a subject has been rightly taught, that when the time comes round for taking it up again for a further period and it is recalled to mind, it emerges quite differently from what it would have done if it had been badly taught. To make the objection that because the subjects will be forgotten it cannot be right to teach in this way, is to ignore the factors that are at work. We must naturally reckon on being able to forget, for just think of all we should have to carry about in our heads if we could not properly forget and then remember again! The part played by the fact of forgetting, therefore, as well as the actual instruction, must be reckoned with in true education.

This does not mean that it should be a matter for rejoicing whenever children forget. That may safely be left to them! Everything depends on what has passed down into the subconscious regions, in a way that will enable it to be duly recalled. The unconscious belongs to the being of man as well as the conscious. In regard to all these matters we must realize that it is the task of education to appeal both to the whole human being and to his different parts and members. Here, again, it is essential to start from the whole; there must first be comprehension of the whole and then of the parts. But to this end it is also necessary to take one's start from the whole. First we must grasp the whole and then the parts. If in counting we simply place one thing beside another, and add them together, we are leaving out the human being as a whole. But we appeal to the whole human being when we first visualize the sum as a whole and thence proceed to the parts that compose it.

.   .   .   .

The teaching of history is very open to the danger of losing sight of the human being. We have seen that in really fruitful education, everything must be given its right place. The plants must be studied in their connection with the earth and the different animal species in their connection with man. Whatever the subject-matter, the concrete human element must be retained; everything must be related, in some way, to man.

When we begin to teach the child history, we must understand that at the age when it is possible for him to realize the connection of plant-life with the earth and the earth herself as an organism, when he can see in the human being a living synthesis of the whole animal kingdom, he is simply unable to form any idea of so-called causal connections in history. We may teach history very skilfully in the ordinary sense, describing one epoch after another and showing how the first is the cause of the second; we may describe how in the history of art, Michael Angelo followed Leonardo da Vinci, for instance, in a natural sequence of cause and effect. But before the age of twelve, the child simply has no understanding of the working of cause and effect which has become a conventional factor in grown-up historical studies. Just as an unmusical strumming on a piano means nothing to us, so this kind of historical teaching means nothing to the child, and it is only by dint of coercion that he will take it in at all. It has the same effect on his soul as a piece of stone that is swallowed and passes into the stomach. Just as we would never dream of giving the stomach a stone instead of bread, so we must make sure that we nourish the soul not with stones, but with food that it can assimilate. If history and historical life are to be related in a living way to man, the first thing we shall have to do is to awaken a conception of time which is connected with the human being himself.

We might have three history books, the first dealing with antiquity, the second with the Middle Ages, and the third with our modern age, but there would be little enough of an historical conception of time in them. But suppose I began by saying to the child: "You are now ten years old, so you were alive in the year 1913. Your father is much older than you and he was alive in the year 1890; his father, again, was alive in 1850. Now imagine that you are standing here and stretching your arm back to someone who represents your father; he stretches his arm back to his father (your grandfather)—now you have reached the year 1850." The child then begins to realize that approximately one century is represented by three or four generations. The line of generations running backwards from the twentieth century brings him finally to his very early ancestors. Thus the sixtieth generation back leads into the epoch of the birth of Christ. In a large room it might be possible to arrange enough children standing in a line, stretching an arm backwards to each other so that the sixtieth would represent the ancestor living at the time of Christ's nativity. Space is changed, as it were, into time.

If the teacher has a fertile, inventive mind, he can find other ways and means of expressing the same thing—I am merely indicating a principle. In this way the child begins to realize that he himself is part of history; figures like Alfred the Great, Cromwell and others are made to appear as if they themselves were ancestors. The whole of history thus becomes an actual part of life at school when it is presented to the child in the form of a living conception of time.

History must never be separated from the human being. The child must not think of it as so much book-lore. Many people seem to think that history is something contained in books—although of course it is not always quite as bad as that. At all events, we must try by every possible means to awaken a realization that history is living, and that man himself stands within its stream.

When a living conception of time has been awakened, we can begin to imbue history with inner life and soul—just as we did in the case of arithmetic and geometry by unfolding not a dead, but a living perception. There is a great deal of quibbling to-day about the nature of perception, but the whole point is that we must unfold living and not dead perception. In the symmetry-exercises of which I spoke, the soul actually lives in the act of perception. That is living perception. Just as our aim is to awaken a living perception of space, so must all healthy teaching of history given to a child between the ages of nine and twelve be filled with an element proceeding—in this case—not from the qualities of space but from within from the qualities of heart and soul.

The history lessons must be permeated through and through with a quality proceeding from the heart. And so we must present it as far as possible in the form of pictures. Figures, real forms must stand there and they must never be described in a cold, prosaic way. Without falling into the error of using them as examples for moral or religious admonition, our descriptions must, nevertheless, be coloured with both morality and religion. History must above all lay hold of the child's life of feeling and will. He must be able to enter into a personal relationship with historical figures and with the modes of life prevailing in the various historical epochs. Nor need we confine ourselves merely to descriptions of human beings. We may, for instance, describe the life of some town in the twelfth century, but everything we say must enter the domains of feeling and will in the child. He must himself be able to live in the events, to form himself within them by the way they rouse his own sympathies and antipathies. His life of feeling and will must be stimulated.

This will show you that just into the teaching of history the element of art must everywhere enter. The element of art comes into play when—as I often describe it—a true economy is exercised in teaching. This economy can be exercised if the teacher has thoroughly mastered his subject-matter before he goes into the classroom, if it is no longer necessary for him to ponder over anything because, if rightly prepared, it is there plastically before his soul. He must be so well prepared that the only thing still to be done is the artistic moulding of his lesson. The problem of teaching is thus not merely a question of the pupil's interest, diligence and devotion, but first and foremost of the teacher's interest, diligence and devotion.

No lesson should be given that has not previously been a matter of deep experience in the spirit of the teacher. Obviously, therefore, the organization of the body of teachers must be such that every teacher is given ample time to enter with full and intense experience into the lessons he has to give.

It is a dreadful thing to see a teacher walking round among his pupils, he with a book in his hands, but they having to wrestle with the subject-matter. Those who do not realize how contrary such a thing is to all true principles of education, do not know what is going on unconsciously in the souls of the children, nor do they realize the terrible effect of this unconscious experience. If we give history lessons in school from note-books, the child comes to a certain definite conclusion—not consciously, but unconsciously. It is an unconscious, intellectual conclusion, but it is deeply rooted in his organism: "Why should I learn all these things? The teacher himself doesn't know them, for he has to read from notes. I can do that too, later on, so there is no need for me to learn them first." The child does not, of course, come to this conclusion consciously, but as a matter of fact, when judgments are rooted in the unconscious life of heart and feeling, they have all the greater force. The lessons must pulsate with inner vitality and freshness proceeding from the teacher's own being. When he is describing historical figures, for instance, the teacher should not have first to make an effort before he can remember dates. I have already spoken of the way in which we should convey a conception of time by a picture of the successive generations. Another element, too, must pervade in particular the teaching of history; it must flow forth with elemental power from the teacher himself. Nothing must be abstract; the teacher himself, as a human being, must be the vital factor.

It has been said many times that education should work upon the being of man as a whole and not merely on one part of his nature. Important as it is to consider what the child ought to learn and whether we are primarily concerned with his intellect or his will, the question of the teacher's work is equally important. When it is a matter of educating the whole nature and being of man, the teacher must himself be "man" in the full sense of the word, that is to say, not one who teaches and works merely on the basis of mechanical memory or mechanical knowledge, but who teaches out of his own being, his full manhood. That is the great essential.

X

PHYSICS, CHEMISTRY, HANDWORK, LANGUAGE, RELIGION

From what I have said about the way in which we should teach the child about nature, about plant and animal, I think you will have realized that the aim of the Waldorf School is to relate educational methods to the evolutionary principles and forces as they are active in the successive stages of the child's development. I have already spoken of the significant turning-point occurring between the ninth and tenth year. Only now does the child begin to distinguish himself from the world. Before this age there is no sense of separation in his life of thought and feeling between himself and the phenomena of the outer world. Up to the ninth year, therefore, we must speak of plants, animals, mountains, rivers and so on, in the language of fairy-tales, appealing above all to the child's fantasy. The animals, plants, springs must speak, so that the same kind of being the child is first aware of in himself also in some sense sounds forth to him from out of the external world.

If you will bear in mind the way in which at this age we lead on to botany and zoology, you will realize that the aim of the teaching is to bring the child into a true relationship with the world around him. He learns to know the plants in their connection with the earth, and studies them all from this point of view. The earth becomes a living being who brings forth the plants, just as the human head through a vital principle within it brings forth hair—only, of course, the forms contained in the earth—the plants—have a much richer life and variety. This relationship with the plant world and with the whole earth is of great value to the well-being of the child in body and soul. If we teach him to see man as a synthesis of the animal species spread fan-like over the earth, we help to bring him into a true relationship with other living beings standing below him in the scale of creation. Until the age of eleven or twelve, the mainspring of all nature-study should be the relation of the human being to the world.

Then comes the age when, for the first time, we may draw the child's attention to processes going on in the outer world independently of man. Between the eleventh and twelfth year, and not until then, we may begin to teach about the minerals and stones. The plants as they grow out of the earth are in this sense related to stone and mineral. Earlier teaching about the mineral kingdom in any other form than this utterly spoils the child's inner mobility of soul. That which has no relationship with man is mineral in its nature. We should only begin to deal with the mineral kingdom when the child has properly found his own place in the world—when in thought and especially in feeling he has grasped the life of the plants and his will has been strengthened by a true conception of the animals—the two kingdoms of nature which are nearest to him.

What applies to the minerals applies equally to physics and chemistry, as also to all so-called causal connections in history and geography—in short, to all processes that must be studied in separation from man. Study of the great historical connections that cannot be directly related to the human being in the sense of which I spoke yesterday, should be postponed until the period beginning between the eleventh and twelfth years. Only from now on can one begin a study of what first of all has little to do with man.

The right age for a child to begin his school life is when he gets his second teeth—at about the seventh year. Until then, school is not really the place for him; if we have to take a child before this age, all kinds of compromises are necessary. I will try, however, to explain certain basic principles. When the child first comes to school, we teach him in such a way that as yet he makes no distinction or separation between himself and the world at large. Between the ninth and tenth year we begin to awaken a living intelligence through a knowledge of the plants, and to strengthen his will through a knowledge of the animals. In mineralogy, physics, and chemistry we can only work upon the intellect, and then—as a necessary counterbalance—art must be introduced. (I shall be speaking more of this in to-morrow's lecture.) From the eleventh or twelfth year onwards we shall find that the child is able to form a rational, intellectual conception of cause and effect and this must now be elaborated in physics and chemistry. These processes, which should gradually lead to the study of astronomy, must not, however, be explained to the child before he has reached the age of eleven or twelve. If we describe simple chemical processes—combustion, for instance—before this age, our descriptions must be purely pictorial and imaginative, without any reference to the thought-connections between cause and effect. This should not be introduced until the child has reached a point between the ages of eleven and twelve. The less we speak of causality before this age, the stronger, the more vital and also more truly inward will the soul become; if, on the other hand, we speak of causality to a younger child, dead concepts, and even dead feelings will pass with a withering effect into his soul.

The aim of the Waldorf School methods of education has been throughout to create the plan of work out of the human being. In every detail we take the different life-periods into consideration and arrange the lessons given in the classes according to the needs of human nature itself. On the other hand it is altogether our intention to enable our children to enter the life of the world in the right way. To achieve this we must lead over from physics and chemistry to various forms of practical work when the child has reached the fourteenth and fifteenth year. In the classes for children of this age, therefore, we have introduced hand-spinning and, weaving—for through these things one enters intelligently into practical life. Our pupils learn spinning and weaving and get to know something of how these things are done in a factory. They should also have some knowledge of elementary technical chemistry, the preparation and manufacture of colours and the like.

During their school life children ought to acquire really practical ideas of their environment. The affairs of ordinary life often remain quite unintelligible to many people to-day because the teaching they receive at school does not lead over, at the right moment, from the essentially human to the practical activities of life and the world in general. In a certain direction this is bound to injure the whole development of the soul. Think, for a moment, of the sensitiveness of the human body to some element in the air, for instance, which the organism cannot assimilate. In the social life of the world, of course, conditions are not quite the same. In social life we are forced to put up with many incongruities, but we can adapt ourselves if at the right age and in the right way we have been introduced into them.

Just think how many people nowadays get into a tram without having the faintest idea of the principles governing its motion and mechanism. Or they see a railway every day and have absolutely no notion of the machinery of a locomotive! This means that they are surrounded on all hands by inventions and creations of the human mind with which they have no contact at all. It is the beginning of unsocial life simply to accept these creations and inventions of the mind of man without understanding them, in a general way, at any rate. At the Waldorf School, therefore, when the children are fourteen or fifteen years old, we begin to give instruction and actual experience in matters that play a rôle in practical life. This age of adolescence is nowadays regarded from a very limited, one-sided point of view. The truth is, that at puberty the human being opens out to the world. Hitherto he has lived more within himself, but he is now ready to understand his fellow-men and the things of the world. Hence, to concentrate before puberty on all that relates man to nature, is to act in accordance with true principles of human development, but at the age of fourteen or fifteen we must with all energy begin to connect the children with the creations and inventions of the human mind. This will enable them to understand and find their right place in social life. If educators had adhered to this principle some sixty or seventy years ago, the so-called "Social Movement" of to-day would have taken quite a different form in Europe and America. Tremendous progress has been made in technical and commercial efficiency during the last sixty or seventy years. Great progress has been made in technical skill, national trade has become world trade, and finally a world-economy has arisen from national economies. In the last sixty or seventy years the outer configuration of social life has entirely changed, yet our mode of education has continued as if nothing had happened. We have utterly neglected to acquaint our children with the practical affairs of the world at the time when this should be done—namely, at the age of fourteen or fifteen.

At the Waldorf School we are not so narrow-minded as to look down in any way on higher classical education—for in many respects it is extremely beneficial; we prepare pupils whose parents desire it, or who desire it themselves, both for a higher classical education and for final certificates and diplomas. But we do not forget how necessary it is for our age to understand the reason that induced the Greeks—whose one purpose in education was to serve the ends of practical life—not to spend all their time learning Egyptian, a language belonging to the far past, whereas we make a special point of familiarizing our boys—and girls too—with a world not of the present but of the past. What wonder that human beings as a rule have so little understanding of how to live in the world of the present!

The world's destiny has grown beyond man's control simply because education has not kept pace with the changing conditions of social life. In the Waldorf School we follow our feeling that it is indeed possible to develop the human being to full manhood and help him to find his right place in the ranks of humanity.

. . . .

Our aim is to develop the child in such a way that he may later reveal the qualities of full manhood and be able also to find his true place in the world, and this must be our first consideration in the teaching of languages.

As far as the mother-tongue is concerned, of course, the teaching is adapted to the age of the child; it is given in the form I have already described in connection with other lessons. An outstanding feature, however, is that at the Waldorf School we begin to teach the child two foreign languages, French and English, directly he comes to school, at the age of six or seven. By this means we endeavour to give our children something that will be more and more necessary to the human being in the future. To understand the purely human aspect of the teaching of languages we must remember that the faculty of speech is rooted in the very depths of man's being. The mother-tongue is so deeply rooted in the breathing system, the blood circulation and in the configuration of the vascular system, that the child is affected not only in spirit and soul, but in spirit, soul, and body by the way in which this mother-tongue comes to expression within him. We must realize, however, that the different languages in the world permeate man and bring the human element to expression in quite different ways. In the case of primitive languages this is quite obvious; it is also true of the more civilized languages, though this often escapes recognition.

Now among European languages there is one that proceeds purely from the element of feeling. Although in the course of time intellectualism has seized the element of pure feeling, feeling is nevertheless the basis of this particular language; hence the elements of intellect and will are less firmly implanted in the human being through the language itself. By a study of other languages, then, the elements of will and intellect must be unfolded. Again, we have a language that emanates particularly from the element of plastic fantasy—everything is, as it were, present in the configuration of the sounds themselves. Because this is so, the child acquires an innately plastic, innately formative power as he learns to speak. Another language in civilized Europe is rooted paramountly in the element of will. Its very cadences, the structure of its vowels and consonants reveal that this is so. When people speak, it is as though they were driving back waves of the sea with the out-breathed air. The element of will is living in the language here.

Other languages call forth in man to a greater extent the elements of feeling, music, imagination. In short, each different language is related to the human being in a particular way.

You will say that I ought to name these various languages, but I purposely avoid doing so, because we have not reached the point of being able to face the civilized world so objectively that we can bear the whole impersonal truth of these things!

From what I have said about the character of the different languages, you will realize that the effects produced on the nature of man by one particular genius of speech must be balanced by the effects of another—if, that is to say, our aim is a really human and not a specialized, national development of man. This is the reason why at the Waldorf School we begin with three languages, even in the case of the very youngest children; a great deal of time, moreover, is devoted to this subject.

It is good to begin teaching foreign languages at this early age, because up to the point lying between the ninth and tenth years the child still bears within him something of the quality characteristic of the first period of life from birth to the time of the change of teeth. During these years the child is pre-eminently an imitative being. He learns his mother tongue wholly by imitation. Without much claim being made on the intellect, the child imitates the language spoken around him, and learns, at the same time, not only the outer sounds and tones of speech, but also the inner, musical, soul element of the language. His first language is acquired—if I may be allowed the expression—as a finer kind of habit which passes into the depths of his whole being.

When the child comes to school after the time of the change of teeth, the teaching of languages appeals more to the soul and less strongly to the bodily nature. Nevertheless, up to the ages of nine and ten the child still brings with him a sufficient faculty of imaginative imitation to enable us to mould the teaching of a language in such a way that it will be absorbed by his whole being, not merely by the forces of soul and spirit.

This is why it is of such far-reaching importance not to let the first three years of school-life slip by without any instruction in foreign languages. On purely educational principles we begin to teach foreign languages in the Waldorf School directly the child enters the elementary classes.

I need hardly say that the teaching of languages is closely adapted to the different ages.... In our days men's thinking, as far as realities are concerned, has become chaotic. They imagine themselves firmly rooted in reality because of their materialism, but in point of fact they are theorists. Those who flatter themselves on being practical men of the world are eminently theorists; they get it into their heads that something or other is right, without really shaping it out of practical life. And so, especially in education and teaching, they fall with an utterly impracticable radicalism into the opposite extreme when anything has been found wrong. It has been realized that when the old method of teaching languages, especially Latin and Greek, is based entirely on grammar and rules of syntax, the lessons tend to become mechanical and external. And so exactly the opposite principle has been introduced simply because people cannot think consistently. They see that something is wrong and fall into the other extreme, imagining that this will put it right. The consequence is that they now work on the principle of teaching no grammar at all. This again is irrational, for it means nothing else than that in some particular branch of knowledge the human being is left at the stage of mere consciousness and not allowed to advance to self-consciousness. Between the ninth and tenth year the child passes from the stage of consciousness to that of self-consciousness. He distinguishes himself from the world.

This is the age when we can begin—gradually, of course—to teach the rules of grammar and syntax, for the child is now reaching a point where he thinks not only about the world, but about himself as well. To think about oneself means—as far as speech is concerned—to be able not merely to speak instinctively, but to apply rational rules in speech. It is nonsense, therefore, to teach languages without grammar of any kind. If we avoid all rules, we cannot impart to the child the requisite inner firmness for his tasks in life. It is all-important to bear in mind, on the other hand, that the child only passes willingly from consciousness to self-consciousness between the ages of nine and ten. To teach grammar before this age, therefore, is absolutely irrational.

We must know when the change occurs between the ninth and tenth years in order to lead over gradually from an instinctive, direct acquiring of language to the rational element of grammar. This applies to the mother tongue as well. Real injury is done to the child's soul if he is crammed with rules of grammar or syntax before this eventful moment in his life. Previously, the teaching must appeal to instinct and habit through his faculty of imitation. It is the task of speech to inaugurate self-consciousness between the ninth and tenth year—and as a rule self-consciousness comes to light in grammar and syntax. This will show you why, at the Waldorf School, we make use of the two or three preceding years, in order to introduce the teaching of languages at the right age and in accordance with the laws of human development.

You see now how Waldorf School education aims, little by little, at enabling the teacher to read, not in a book and not according to the rules of some educational system, but in the human being himself. The Waldorf School teacher must learn to read man—the most wonderful document in all the world. What he gains from this reading grows into deep enthusiasm for teaching and education. For only what is contained in the book of the world can stimulate the all-round activity of body, soul, and spirit that is necessary only in the teacher. All other study, all other books and reading, should be a means enabling the teacher ultimately to read the great book of the world. If he can do this he will teach with the necessary enthusiasm—and enthusiasm alone can generate the force and energy of impulse that bring life into a classroom.

. . . .

The principle of the "universal human", which I have described in its application to the different branches of teaching, is expressed in Waldorf School education in that this school does not in any sense promulgate any particular philosophy or religious conviction. In this connection it has, of course, been absolutely essential—above all in an art of education derived from Anthroposophy—to remove from the Waldorf School any accusation of being an "anthroposophical school". Most emphatically it can be nothing of the kind. New efforts must be made every day to avoid falling into anthroposophical bias—shall I say—on account possibly of over-enthusiasm or honest conviction on the part of the teachers. The conviction, of course, is there in the Waldorf teachers because they are anthroposophists. But the fundamental question of the Waldorf School education is the human being himself, not the human being as an adherent of any particular philosophy.

And so—with the various religious bodies in mind—we were willing to come to a compromise demanded by the times and in the early days to confine our attention to the methods to be adopted in a "universal human" education. To begin with, all religious instruction was left in the hands of the pastors of the various denominations—Catholic teaching to Catholic priests, Protestant teaching to Protestant ministers. But a great many pupils in the Waldorf School are "dissenters"—as we say in Central Europe—that is to say they are children who would receive no religious instruction at all if this were limited to Catholic and Protestant teaching. The Waldorf School was originally founded for the children of working people in connection with a certain business, although for a long time now it has been a school for all classes of the community—and for this reason a large majority of the children belonged to no religious confession. As often happens in schools in Central Europe, these children were being taught nothing in the way of religion, and so, for their sake, we have introduced a so-called "free" religious instruction. We make no attempt to introduce theoretical Anthroposophy into the School. Such a thing would be utterly false. Anthroposophy so far has been given for grown-up people; one speaks of Anthroposophy to grown-up people, and its ideas and conceptions are therefore clothed in a form suitable for them. Simply to take what is destined for grown-up people in anthroposophical literature and introduce that, would have been to distort the whole principle of Waldorf School education. In the case of children who have been handed over to us voluntarily for free religious instruction, the whole point has been to recognize from their age what we should give them in the way of religious instruction.

Let me repeat once again that the religious teaching given at the Waldorf School—and corresponding services are connected with it—is not in any sense an attempt to introduce an anthroposophical conception of the world. The ages of the children are always taken into fullest account. As a matter of fact the great majority of the children attend, although we have made it a strict rule only to admit them if their parents wish it. Since the element of pure pedagogy plays an important and essential part in this free religious teaching—which is, of course, Christian in the deepest sense —parents who wish their children to be educated in a Christian way, and also according to the Waldorf School principles, send them to us. As I say, the teaching is Christian through and through, and the effect of it is that the whole School is pervaded by a deeply Christian atmosphere. Our religious instruction makes the children realize the significance of all the great Christian festivals, of the Christmas and Easter festivals, for instance, much more deeply than is usually the case nowadays.

The ages of the children must always be taken into account in any teaching connected with religion, for infinite harm is wrought if ideas and conceptions are conveyed prematurely. In the Waldorf School the child is led, first of all, to an understanding of universal Divinity in the world. You will remember that when the child first comes to school between the ages of seven and ten, we let plants, clouds, springs, and the like, speak for themselves. The child's whole environment is living and articulate. From this we can readily lead on to the universal Father-Principle imminent in the world. When the rest of the teaching takes the form I have described, the child is well able to conceive that all things have a divine origin.

And so we form a link with the knowledge of nature conveyed to the child in the form of fantasy and fairy-tales. Our aim in so doing is to awaken in him, first of all, a sense of gratitude for everything that happens in the world. Gratitude for what human beings do for us, and also for the gifts vouchsafed by nature—this is what will guide religious feeling into the right path. To unfold the child's sense of gratitude is of the greatest imaginable significance. It may seem paradoxical, yet it is nevertheless profoundly true, that human beings should learn to feel a certain gratitude when the weather is favourable for some undertaking or another. To be capable of gratitude to the cosmos—even though it can only be in the life of imagination—this will deepen our whole life of feeling in a religious sense.

Love for all creation must then be added to this gratitude. And if we lead the child on to the age of nine or ten in the way described, nothing is easier than to reveal in the living world around him qualities he must learn to love. Love for every flower, for sunshine, for rain—this again will deepen perception of the world in a religious sense. If gratitude and love have been unfolded in the child before the age of ten, we can then proceed to develop a true sense and understanding of duty. Premature development of the sense of duty by dint of commands and injunctions will never lead to a religious inwardness.

He who would educate in the sense of true Christianity must realize that before the age of nine or ten it is not possible to convey to the child's soul an understanding of what the Mystery of Golgotha brought into the world, or of all that is connected with the personality and divinity of Christ Jesus. The child is exposed to great dangers if we have failed to introduce the principle of universal divinity before this age, and by universal divinity I mean the divine Father-Principle. We must show the child how divinity is imminent in all nature, in all human evolution, how it lives and moves not only in the stones, but in the hearts of other men, in their every act. The child must be taught, by the natural authority of the teacher, to feel gratitude and love for this universal divinity. In this way, the basis for a right attitude to the Mystery of Golgotha just between the ninth and tenth years is laid down.

You see now why it is of such infinite importance to understand the being of man from the aspect of his development in time. Try for a moment to realize what a difference there is if we teach a seven- or eight-year-old child about the New Testament, or—having first stimulated a consciousness of universal divinity in the whole of nature—wait until he has reached the age of nine-and-a-half or ten before we pass to the New Testament as such. In the latter case, right preparation has been made and the Gospels will live in all their supersensible greatness. If we teach the younger child about the New Testament it will not lay hold of his whole being, but will remain mere phraseology, just so many rigid, prosaic concepts. The consequent danger is that religious feeling will harden in the child and continue through life in a rigid form, instead of in a living form which through and through pervades his feeling for the world. We prepare the child most beautifully to take into himself from the ninth and tenth years onwards, the glory of Christ Jesus if, before this age, he has been introduced to the principle of universal Divinity imminent in the whole world.

This, then, is the aim of the religious teaching given at the Waldorf School to an ever-increasing number of children whose parents wish it. The teaching is based on the purely human element and associated, moreover, with a certain form of ritual. A service is held every Sunday for the children who are given this free religious instruction, and for those who have left school a service with a different ritual is held. A certain ritual, then, similar in many respects to the Mass, but always adapted to the age of the child, is associated with the religious teaching given at the Waldorf School.

Now it was very difficult to introduce into this religious instruction the principle it is our aim to unfold in the Waldorf School, the principle of the development of man as such, for in religious matters to-day people are least of all inclined to relinquish their own special line. We hear a great deal of talk about a "universal human" religion, but the opinion of almost everyone is influenced by the views of the particular religious body to which he belongs. If we rightly understand the task of humanity in days to come, we shall realize that the free religious teaching that has been inaugurated by the Waldorf School is a true assistance to this task.

Anthroposophy as given to grown-up people is naturally not introduced into the Waldorf School. Rather do we regard it as our task to imbue our teaching with something for which man thirsts and longs: a realization of the Divine, of the Divine in nature and in human history, arising from a true conception of the Mystery of Golgotha.

This end is also served when the whole teaching has the necessary quality and colouring. I have already said that the teacher must come to a point where all his work is a moral deed, where he regards the lessons themselves as a kind of divine office. This can only be achieved if it is possible to introduce the elements of moral instruction and religion into the school for those who desire it, and we have made this attempt in the religious instruction given at the Waldorf School—in so far as social conditions permit to-day. In no sense do we work towards a blind, rationalistic Christianity, but towards a true understanding of the Christ Impulse in the evolution of mankind. Our one and only aim is to give the human being something that he still needs, even if all his other teaching has endowed him with the qualities of full manhood. Even if this be so, even if full manhood has been unfolded through all the other teaching, a religious deepening is still necessary if the human being, in an all-round way, is to find a place in the world befitting his inborn spiritual nature. To develop and unfold the whole man and deepen him in a religious sense—this we have tried to regard as one of the most essential tasks of Waldorf School education.

XI

Memory, Temperaments, Bodily Culture and Art

There are two sides to be considered in teaching and education. One side is connected with the subject-matter of the lessons, and the other with the child whose faculties it is our task to unfold, in accordance with what we learn from a true observation of the human being. If we adopt the methods described in these lectures, our teaching will always appeal to the particular faculties that should be unfolded during the different life-periods. Very special attention, however, must be paid to the development of the child's memory. Now here it must be realized that, on account of a deficient understanding of the being of man, our predecessors have been prone to burden the memories of children and—as I said yesterday in another connection—there has been a reaction from this to the very opposite extreme. The tendency in the most modern systems of education is to eliminate memory almost entirely. Now both methods are wrong. The point is really that the memory ought to be left alone up to the time of the change of teeth, when in the ordinary way the child is sent to school. I have already said that during this period of life, physical body, etheric body, astral body and ego-organization are working in unison. The way in which the child develops in himself, by way of imitation, everything he observes around him, has the effect of stimulating, even in the physical body itself, the forces underlying the development of memory. During these years of his life, therefore, the memory must be left to develop without interference.

From the time of the change of teeth, however, when the element of soul-and-spirit is released from the body in a certain sense, systematic training of the memory is of the greatest importance. Through the whole of a man's life the memory makes claims on his physical body. Unless there is an all-round development of the physical body, the memory will be impaired in some way. Indeed it is well-known to-day that the one or the other injury to the brain at once results in defective memory.

When we are dealing with children, it is not enough to notice that an element of soul is involved in disease. As teachers, we must always be on the alert for every little intimate effect that is being produced on the bodily nature of the child by the soul and spirit. An undue development of memory will injure the child for the whole of life—will even injure his physical body.

How, then, can we rightly unfold the faculty of memory? Above all we must realize that abstract concepts—concepts built up by the rationalizing intellect—are always a load on the memory, specially in the period of life between the change of teeth and puberty. Imaginative, perceptible ideas, however, given vividly in the lessons as I have shown, given in plastic-pictorial form in an artistic teaching, awaken living forces which play right down into the physical body and which allow the memory to unfold in the right way. The very best foundation for the development of memory is to give our teaching in an artistic way during the elementary school age.

Right control of the faculty of bodily movement will always be induced if art is properly taught. If we are able to stimulate the child, however, to self-activity in art, if as he paints, writes, makes music, or draws, his bodily nature bestirs itself together with his qualities of spirit, we shall rightly unfold the forces that must proceed from the soul and come to the aid of memory in the physical body. In to-morrow's lecture I will explain how this is achieved in eurhythmy. We must not fall into the error of believing that a complete elimination or an insufficient feeding of memory can ever be of benefit to the child.

Here are three golden rules for the development of memory: Concepts load the memory; the perceptibly artistic builds it up; activities of will strengthen it and make it firm. We have splendid opportunities for applying these three golden rules if we teach nature-study and history in the way I have been indicating during these lectures. Arithmetic too may be used for the same end, for in arithmetic we ought always to begin with artistic feeling as I have tried to show you. Now when the children thoroughly understand the more simple operations, counting up to ten or twenty, let us say—we need not be afraid of allowing them to memorize the rest. It is not right to overload the child with too many concrete pictures, any more than it is to put too great a strain on his powers of memory, for concepts carried too far into complexity have the same effect. We must therefore carefully observe how the memory is unfolding in the case of each individual child.

Here we see how necessary it is for the teacher and educator to have some understanding of the tendencies to health and disease in the human being. Strange experiences have often come one's way in this connection. A gentleman whose whole thought is concerned with education once came to visit the Waldorf School and I tried to explain the spirit underlying the teaching there. After a little while he said: "Yes, but if you work on those lines the teachers will have to know a great deal about medicine." It seemed to him quite impossible that they could understand medicine to the extent necessary in such a school. I said that even though this would arise naturally out of a knowledge of the nature of man, a certain amount of medical instruction ought to form part of any course for teachers. Questions concerned with health ought not to be left merely to the school doctor. I think we are particularly fortunate at the Waldorf School in that our school doctor himself is on the College of Teachers. Dr. Eugen Kolisko is a doctor by profession and besides looking after the children's health, he is also a member of the teaching staff. In this way everything connected with the bodily health of the children can proceed in fullest harmony with their education.

This, in effect, is necessary: our teachers must learn to

understand matters connected with health and sickness in the child. To give an example: a teacher notices a child growing paler and paler. Another child may lose his natural colour because his face begins to be excessively red. If he observes accurately, the teacher will find that the latter child is showing signs of restlessness and peevishness. All such symptoms must be related to the nature of soul and spirit. Abnormal pallor—or even the mere tendency to it—is the result of over-exertion of the memory. The memory of such a child has been overstrained and one must put a stop to this. In the case of the child with an abnormally high colour, the memory has not been given enough to do. This child must be given things to memorize, and then we must make him show that he has retained them in his mind. The memory of a child who grows paler and paler must therefore be relieved, whereas in the case of a child with excessive colour, we must set about developing the memory.

We only approach the whole human being if we are thus able to handle his nature of soul and spirit in intimate harmony with his physical body. In the Waldorf School, the child, the growing human being, is handled according to his qualities of spirit, soul and body, above all according to his particular temperament.

In the classroom itself, we arrange the children in a way that enables the various temperaments—choleric, sanguine, melancholic or phlegmatic—to be expressed and adjusted amongst themselves. The very best way is to make the choleric children or again the melancholic children sit together, for then they tone each other down. One must of course know how to judge and then deal with the different temperaments, for this in turn affects the very roots of bodily development.

Take the case of a sanguine child, inattentive in his lessons. Every impression coming from the outer world immediately engages his attention but passes away again as quickly. The right treatment for such a child will be to reduce the quantity of sugar in his food—not unduly, of course. The less sugar he absorbs, the more will the excessively sanguine qualities be modified and a harmonized temperament take their place.

In the case of a melancholic child who is always brooding, just the opposite treatment is necessary. More sugar must be added to his food. In this way we work right down into the physical constitution of the liver, for the action of the liver differs essentially according to whether a large or small quantity of sugar is taken. In effect, every activity of outer life penetrates deeply into the physical organism of man.

At the Waldorf School we take the greatest care that there shall be an intimate contact between the teaching staff and the parents of the children. A really intimate contact, of course, is only possible to a certain degree, for it depends on the amount of understanding possessed by the parents. We try, however, to the greatest possible extent, to induce the parents to come to the class-teacher concerned to obtain advice as to the most suitable diet for the individual children. This is just as important as what is taught in the classroom.

We must not imagine, in a materialistic sense, that the body does everything, though obviously a child with no hands cannot be taught to play the piano. The rôle of the body is to be a suitable instrument. Just as one cannot teach a child with deficient hands to play the piano, one cannot rid a child whose liver is over-active, of melancholy—no matter what psychological measures are employed by abstract systems of education. If, however, the action of the liver is regulated by sweetening the child's diet, he will be able to use this bodily organ as a fit instrument. Then and not till then, psychological and spiritual measures will be begin to be effective.

People often imagine that reforms can be introduced into education by the reiteration of abstract principles. All the world knows what is desirable in teaching and how education ought to proceed. Yet true education demands an understanding of the human being that can only be acquired little by little, and so—although I neither attack nor belittle the knowledge possessed by nearly everyone on the subject of education—I say that it is of no practical use. This kind of knowledge seems to me just like someone who says: "I want a house built; it must look nice, be comfortable and weatherproof. . . ." And then off he goes to someone who merely knows that the house must have all these qualities, and thinks he can set about building. But to know these things is of no practical use. That is approximately as much as people in general know about the art of education, and yet they think they can bring about reforms. If I want a house properly built, I must go to an architect who knows in detail how the plan must be drawn, how the bricks are to be laid, how massive the girders must be to bear the weight upon them and so on. The essential thing is to know in detail how the human being is constituted, and not to speak vaguely about human nature in general as one speaks about a house being weatherproof, comfortable and beautiful to look at.

The civilized world must realize that technique—a spiritualized technique of course—is necessary in every detail of the art of education. If it becomes general, this realization will indeed be a boon to all the very praiseworthy efforts in the direction of educational reform that are being made to-day.

. . . .

The significance of these principles is revealed above all when we come to consider the very different individualities of children. It has sometimes been the practice in schools not to allow children who cannot keep up with the work in a particular class to go on to the next. Now in an art of education where the child is taught in accordance with his particular age of life, it must gradually become out of the question to leave a child behind in a class, for then he will fall out of the sequence of the kind of teaching that is suited to his years. In the Waldorf School, of course, each class consists of children of one particular age. If, therefore, a child who ought to go up to the fourth class is left behind in the third, the inner course of his education comes into variance with his age. As far as we can, we avoid this in the Waldorf School. Only in very exceptional cases it happens that a child stays behind in his class. We make every effort to handle each child-individuality in such a way that it will not be necessary for him to stay behind.

For this, however, something else is certainly required. As you all know, there are children who do not develop normally, who are in some way abnormal. At the Waldorf School we have instituted a special "helping" class for these children. This helping class provides for children whose faculties of thinking, feeling or willing are under-developed, and it has become very dear to our hearts. A child whom we cannot have in a class because of a weakness of some power of soul is taken into this separate class. And it is really delightful at the Waldorf School to find a kind of competition among the staff of teachers arising round a child, when it is found necessary to move him from his normal class into the helping class. After all I have been saying, you will realize that there is the greatest harmony between the members of the teaching staff at the Waldorf School, but there is always a certain struggle when such a thing has to be done. It means that Dr. Karl Schubert—a man so rich in blessing for this work—to whom the helping class had been entrusted, has to face a regular onset! The teachers never like giving up a child to him. The children, too, feel it rather against the grain to have to leave their normal class and the teacher whom they love, to go into the helping class. But again it is a blessing that before very long they do not want to leave the helping class because they have such a love for Dr. Schubert. He is extraordinarily well-fitted to have charge of this helping class on account of his qualities of character, temperament, and his infinite capacity of love. This capacity of love, devotion and unselfishness—and they are really the foundation of the art of teaching—are specially needed, when it is a matter of bringing on children in an isolated class of this kind to a point where they can again return to the class corresponding to their age, and this is the goal we set ourselves, with the aid of the helping class.

True knowledge of the nature of man brings the following facts to light. It is really nonsense to speak of abnormalities or disease of the spiritual part of man's being—although of course in colloquial language and for the purposes of everyday life there is no need to be fanatical and pedantic about such matters. Fundamentally speaking, the spirit and the soul are never ill. Illness can only occur in the bodily foundation and what then passes over from the body into the soul. Since the human being in earthly existence can only be handled by approaching his nature of spirit and soul through the body, it is essential in the treatment of so-called abnormal children to realize that the body, because of its abnormality, is making it impossible to approach the being of soul and spirit. The difficulty lies in the body. As soon as we overcome a bodily defect or a defect of body and soul in the child and are able to approach his nature of soul and spirit, we have done what is necessary. In this connection, therefore, our constant aim must be to understand and recognize the delicate, intimate qualities and forces of the bodily nature of man.

If we observe that a child does not grasp things normally, that something hampers him from connecting concepts and perceptions, we shall have to conclude that there is some irregularity in the nervous system. Individual treatment will do much in such a case, perhaps by going more slowly in the teaching, or stimulating the nature of will and the like. When a child is abnormal, our treatment must always be individual and we shall do unspeakable good by such measures as I have indicated—perhaps by teaching slowly or stimulating the element of will into greater activity. Great attention, of course, must be paid to bodily training and culture in the case of such a child. Let me explain certain principles by giving you a simple example.

Suppose it is difficult for a child to combine ideas in his mind. We shall achieve much by giving the child physical exercises in which, out of his inner man, he must bring his own body, his whole organic system into a co-ordinating movement. We may tell him, for instance, to touch the lobe of his left ear with the third finger of the right hand and make him do the exercise quickly. Then we may tell him to touch the top of his head with the little finger of the left hand and alternate the first and second exercises quickly, one after the other. The organism is brought into movement in such a way that the child's thoughts must flow swiftly into the movements he makes. Thus by stimulating the nervous system we make it into a good foundation for the faculty which the child must exercise when it is a question of connecting or separating ideas, perceptions.

Really wonderful experiences can show us how the spiritual nature of the child may be stimulated by the culture of the body. Suppose, for example, a child returns again and again to one fixed idea. This tendency is obviously a great weakness in his soul. He simply cannot help repeating certain words or returning over and over again to the same ideas. They take a deep hold of his being and he cannot get rid of them. If we observe such a child closely, we shall generally find that he walks too much on his heels and not with the toes and the front part of the foot. (All these symptoms, of course, take an individual form in each child and that is why a true knowledge of the human being—one that can make individual distinctions—is so necessary.) Such a child must do movements where he must first pay attention to every step he takes and repeat them until they gradually become a habit. And then, if it is not too late—as a matter of fact a great deal can be achieved in this direction between the seventh and twelfth year—we shall see an extraordinary improvement in the inner defect of the child's soul. We must, however, understand the way in which movements of fingers of the right hand let us say, work on the speech-organism, how movements of fingers on the left hand work upon the forces which proceed from the faculty of thinking and come to the assistance of this speech-organism. We must know too how walking on the toes or walking on the heels reacts upon the faculties of speech and thought, and specially on the will. The art of eurhythmy, working as it does with normal forces, teaches us a great deal when we come to deal with the abnormal. The movements of eurhythmy—which are of course primarily of the nature of art when carried out by the normal human being—are then modified in such a way that they have a therapeutic effect. Since the movements are derived from laws of the human organism itself, the faculties of spirit and soul—which can still be always aroused during the period of growth—are given an impulse that proceeds from the bodily nature. This proves how very necessary it is to realize the unison between spirit, soul and body when we have to deal with abnormal children at school.

The excellent course of teaching that is being developed by Dr. Schubert in this branch of work at the Waldorf School is achieving really splendid results. A great power of love and unselfishness is of course necessary when it is a matter of individual treatment in every case. These qualities are absolutely essential in the helping class. In many directions, too, resignation is required if any results at all are to be achieved, for one can only work with what is there or can be brought out of the human being. If only a quarter or a half of what would make the child absolutely normal is attained, the parents are still apt not to be quite satisfied. But the essential thing in all human action that is guided and directed by the spirit is to be independent of outer recognition, and to become more and more deeply aware of the sustaining power that grows from a sense of inner responsibility. This power will increase step by step in an art of education that perceives, even in these intimate details of life, the harmony between the child's spirit, soul and body. Insight, perception, observation—these are what the teacher needs first of all; if he has these qualities, speech itself will come to life in his whole being. Quite instinctively he will carry over into his practical teaching in an artistic way what he has learnt from observation of the human being.

At a certain age, as I told you yesterday, the child must be led on from the plant- and animal-lore which he grasps more with his faculties of soul, to mineralogy, physics and chemistry, where greater claims are made on his conceptual faculties and intellect, though it is all important that these subjects shall not be taught too soon. During this period of life when we are conveying the idea of causality to the child and he learns of cause and effect in nature, it is essential to balance the inorganic, lifeless elements in nature-study by leading him into the domain of art.

If we are to introduce art to the child in the right way, not only must all our teaching be artistic from the beginning, but art itself must play its proper part in education. That the plastic arts are cultivated you can see if only from the fact that the writing lessons begin with a kind of painting. Thus, according to the Waldorf School principle, we begin to give painting and drawing lessons at a very tender age of childhood. Modelling too is cultivated as much as possible, albeit only from the ninth or tenth year and in a primitive way. It has a wonderfully vitalizing effect on the child's physical sight and on the inner quality of soul in his sight, if, at the right age, he begins to model plastic forms and figures. So many people go through life without even noticing what is most significant in the objects and events of their environment. As a matter of fact, we have to learn how to do it before we can see and observe in the way that gives us our true position in the world. And if the child is to learn to observe aright, it is a very good thing for him to begin, as early as possible, to occupy himself with modelling, to guide what he has seen from his head and eyes into the movements of fingers and hand. In this way we shall not only awaken the child's taste for the artistic around him—in the arrangement of a room, perhaps—and distaste for the inartistic, but he will begin to observe those things in the world which ought to flow into the heart and soul of man.

By beginning musical instruction with song, but leading on more and more to instrumental playing, we develop the element of will in the human being. This musical instruction is not only a means of unfolding his artistic qualities, but also his purely human qualities, especially those of the heart and will. We must of course start with song but pass on as soon as possible to an understanding of instrumental music, in order that the child may learn to distinguish the pure elements of music—rhythm, measure, melody—from everything else, from imitative or pictorial qualities of music and the like. More and more he must begin to realize and experience the purely musical element. By leading the child into the sphere of art, by building a bridge from play to life through art, we can begin, between the eleventh and twelfth year—and that is the proper time—to teach him to understand art. In the principles of education which it is the aim of the Waldorf School to fulfil, it is of vital importance for the child to acquire some understanding of art at the right age. At the age when the child must realize that nature is ruled by abstract law to be grasped by the reason, when he must learn in physics the link between cause and effect in given cases, we must promote an understanding of art as a necessary counter-balance. The child must realize how the several arts have developed in the different epochs of human history, how this or that motif in art plays its part in a particular epoch. Only so will those elements which a human being needs for all-round unfoldment of his being be truly stimulated. In this way too, we can unfold the qualities which, as I shall show in to-morrow's lecture, are essential in moral instruction.

If he acquires an understanding of art, the relation of the human being to his fellow-men will be quite different from what it could be without such understanding. For what is the essence of understanding the world, my dear friends? It is to be able, at the right moment, to reject abstract concepts in order to attain insight into and true understanding of the world.

The mineral kingdom can be understood in the light of cause and effect. The physical can be grasped in this way. When we come to the plant-world, however, it is impossible to grasp everything through logic, reason and intellect. The plastic faculties of man's being must here come into play, for concepts and ideas have to pass into pictures. Any plastic skill that we develop in the child helps him to understand the formations contained in the plants. The animal kingdom can only be comprehended if the ideas for its understanding are first implanted and developed in us by moral education. This alone will activate such inner powers as enable us to understand the forces building up the animal structure from the invisible world. How few people, how few physiologists to-day know whence the form of an animal is derived! As a matter of fact the origin of the animal form comes out of the structure of those organs which, in man, become the organs of speech and of song. That is the centre of the origin of the forms and structure of the animal. The animal does not come to the point of articulate speech; it only comes to the point of song as we know it in the birds. In speech and song, form-giving forces stream outwards, giving shape to the air-waves, and sound arises. That which in the organism of speech and song develops from out of a vital principle, passes back into the form of the animal. It is only possible to understand the form of an animal if we realize that it develops, musically as it were, from organs which, at a later stage, are metamorphosed in the human being, into the organic structures connected with the element of music.

To understand man we need an all-round conception of art, for the faculty of reason can only comprehend the inorganic constituents of man's being. If, at the right moment, we know how to lead over the faculty of mental representation to artistic understanding, then, and only then, is a true understanding of man possible. This understanding of man's being must be awakened by the teaching we give on the subject of art. If the teacher himself is possessed of true artistic feeling and can introduce the child to Leonardo's "Last Supper" or Raphael's "Sistine Madonna" at the right age, not only showing the definite relations between the various figures, but how colour, inner perspective and so forth were treated in the time of Leonardo or Raphael—in short, if nature and history alike are imbued with an inner quality of soul through teaching that conveys an understanding of art—then we are bringing the human element into all education.

Nothing must be left undone in the way of imbuing the child with artistic feeling at the right age in life. Our civilization will never receive an impulse of ascent until more art is introduced into the schools. Not only must the whole teaching be permeated with the artistic, but a living understanding of art, called into being by the teacher's own creative power, must set up a counter-balance to all prosaic conceptions of nature and of history.

We deem this an all-essential part of Waldorf School education. True indeed it is—and every genuine artist has felt the same—that art is not a mere discovery of man, but a domain wherein the secrets of nature are revealed to him at a level other than that of ordinary intelligence—a domain where he gazes into the mysteries of the whole universe. Not until the moment when man realizes the world itself to be a work of art, and regards nature as a creative artist—not until then is he ready for a deepening of his being in the religious sense. There is deep meaning in these words of a German poet: "Only through the dawn gates of beauty canst thou pass into the realm of knowledge." It is so indeed; when we grasp the whole being of man through art, we generate in man an understanding of the world in its totality also. That is why our aim in education should be to add to what is required by prosaic culture and civilization, the purely human element. To this end, not only must our teaching itself be full of artistic feeling, but an understanding of art must be awakened in the children. In this way, and in this way alone, can such an end by achieved.

Art and science will then lead on to a moral and religious deepening—as we shall see in to-morrow's lecture. But as a preliminary to religious and moral progress, education and teaching must set up this balance: in the one scale lie all those things that lead into prosaic life, that bind men to the earth; in the other scale lie the counterbalancing factors leading to art—factors that enable man at every moment of his life once more to raise artistically, and so lead directly into the spirit, what must first be worked out in the prose of life.

XII

EDUCATION TOWARDS INNER FREEDOM

The fact that we have both boys and girls at the Waldorf School seems to me to serve two purposes. One of these is to shape the teaching according to the needs of the whole being of man, for with boys alone, education will necessarily tend to one-sidedness. The other is to work towards that relationship of human beings to each other required by social life, especially in our times when women have either obtained their own place in the social order or are seeking to obtain it. The art of education originating from the Waldorf School, therefore, reckons with modern strivings of social life in this connection too. Much that would otherwise remain remote from the one sex or the other can be developed when boys and girls are educated together.

The lectures will have shown you that we attach great importance to the fact that the child shall unfold in his whole being—in spirit, soul and body—and not merely in the direction of spirit and soul alone. That is why we engage the children in bodily activity—especially such bodily activity as will enable them to pass out into life with understanding.

During the hand-work lessons in the Waldorf School, you will find boys and girls sitting together, all engaged in knitting and crochet. That this is not unnatural but absolutely natural activity, is proved by the fact that our boys learn to knit and even darn stockings with a certain pleasure. It never occurs to them that such work is unworthy of their manhood! We do not include these things so much for the sake of giving the boys a knowledge of them, as for the sake of an all-round understanding of life. One of the chief faults of our present social conditions is that man has so little understanding of what his fellow men are doing. We must really cease existing as isolated individuals and groups, and face each other with full and complete understanding, and the main point is that this kind of hand-work gives the human being practical skill in many different directions.

Incongruous though it may appear, my opinion is that nobody can be a real philosopher who is not also able, in an emergency, to darn his stockings or mend his clothes! How can he have any intelligent conception of mighty world-mysteries if in case of need he cannot even look after his footwear? We really cannot hope to penetrate in a truly human sense into world-mysteries, if we are absolutely incapable of dealing with what is nearest at hand! I know that this may seem far-fetched, but I do believe that a philosopher ought to have some understanding at all events of how boots are made and the like, for otherwise he will simply be a man of abstractions. This is an extreme example, of course, but I want to indicate that, on the one hand, ascent to the loftiest spirituality and, on the other, descent to bodily culture and treatment must be included in our principles of education.

From this kind of hand-work the children can be led on to actual manual work and to do it with intelligence and understanding. At the proper age—indeed comparatively early—we let our children make toys and playthings for themselves.—You will have seen some in the exhibition here.—They carve toys from wood and in this way too, we bring the element of art into their play.

To lead play gradually over to the creation of artistic forms and then to the practical work of which I have just spoken, is to act in complete harmony with the demands of man's nature. And it is absorbingly interesting to find that the children's plastic, artistic activity turns quite naturally to the making of playthings and toys. Here again we lead over from art *per se* to art as a factor in industrial life. The children are shown how to make simple implements, simple things for use in the house and at the same time learn how to use saws, knives and other tools in joinery and carpentry.

Boys and girls alike love to be in our workrooms, working with knife and saw and other tools, in addition to their ordinary lessons, and are delighted when they succeed in making something really useful. In this way we stimulate all their instincts for the practical side of life.—On the one hand, then, we unfold a sense for the practical side of life and on the other, for art.

It is so interesting to find that when the children have learnt something about the human organism, for instance, the plastic formation of the bony system or the form of the muscles—that is to say, when they have been given an artistic conception of the structure and functions of the human body—they will begin to express, again in plastic form, their ideas of the shape of some limb, perhaps—not in any slavish sense of imitation, but with free, creative power. Our children are allowed the greatest freedom even in their practical work and are allowed to follow their own sense of discovery. Their souls create the most wonderful forms when they have learnt to observe certain things in the human being or the animal with a truly artistic feeling for nature.

In this way we so teach that what the children know they know with their whole being. Our civilization is calculated to make men cognize everything with their heads. Ideas rest in the head as upon a couch. The ideas are at rest in the head as though they lay in bed. They are asleep; they only "mean" this or that. We carry them stored up in us as in so many little pigeon-holes and with the rest of our being we are unconcerned in them. At the Waldorf School, the children do not merely "have an idea" in their heads; they feel the idea, for it flows into their whole life of feeling. Their being of soul lives in the sense of the idea, which is not merely a concept but becomes a plastic form. The whole complex of ideas at last becomes human form and figure and in the last resort all this passes over into the will. The child learns to transform what he thinks into actual deed. When this happens we do not find thoughts proceeding in one part of the human being, while the will, situated at another part, is nourished merely by instinct. The human being in such a case is really like a wasp. There are wasps which have a head and then a long stalk, and then below this there comes the rest of the body, and this is really an outer symbol, not of the bodily nature of modern man, but of his nature of soul and spirit. He has a head, then a long stalk and his nature of will is an appendage to this. From the spiritual point of view, human beings present a strange appearance to-day—the head dangles in the air and does not know what to make of its own ideas!

This can be rectified if we help the child at all times to permeate his faculties of cognition with feeling and with will. It has long been recognized by contemporary systems that education has veered into one-sided intellectualism, that the head is dangling in the air, and a beginning has been made on the other side to develop practical skill and dexterity. But this does not really unite the two elements. Their union is only possible when knowledge of itself passes into practical skill, and when practical skill is at the same time permeated with the quality of thought, inner understanding of the soul, and spiritual participation.

On the basis of these principles a bridge may be built to moral and religious education. I have already spoken of this and need only add to-day that everything depends upon giving all the teaching and all bodily, all gymnastic exercises in a form which will make the child feel: my bodily nature is a revelation of spirit and the spirit would fain pour creatively into my body. The child must never feel a separation between spirit and body. The moral and religious elements will then live truly in his life of feeling. The great thing to bear in mind is that between the change of teeth and puberty we must not inculcate morality and religion into the child by means of catechism-precepts but by working upon his feeling and perception through our own authority in connection with this period of life. The child must learn to delight in goodness and to abhor evil—to love the good and hate the wicked. In the history lessons, great historical figures and the impulses connected with the different epochs can be presented in such a way that moral and religious sympathies and antipathies will unfold in the child. And then we achieve something of supreme importance.

After puberty, when the child has reached his fifteenth or sixteenth year, a change takes place in his inner nature, leading him from dependence upon authority to his own sense of freedom and hence to the faculty of independent judgment and insight. Here is something that must claim our most watchful attention in education and teaching. If, before puberty, we have awakened the child's feeling for good and evil, for what is and is not divine, these feelings will arise from his own inner being afterwards. His understanding, intellect, insight and power of judgment are uninfluenced; he can now form independent judgments from out of his own being.

If we start by telling the child that he ought to do this and ought to do that, it all remains with him through his later years and then he will always be thinking that such and such a thing is right and such and such a thing is wrong. Convention will colour everything. Now in true education to-day, the human being should not stand within the conventional but have his own judgment even about morality and religion, and this will unfold naturally if it has not been prematurely engaged.

At the Waldorf School we allow the child of fourteen or fifteen to find his own feet in life. We put him really on a par with ourselves. He unfolds his judgment but he still looks back to the authority which we represented, and retains the affection he had for us when we were his teachers. His power of judgment has not been fettered if we have merely worked upon his life of feeling. And so, when the child has reached the age of fourteen or fifteen, we leave his nature of soul and spirit in freedom and, in the higher classes, appeal to his own power of judgment and insight. This freedom in life cannot be achieved by inculcating morality and religion in a dogmatic, canonical fashion but by working simply and solely on the child's powers of feeling and perception at the right age—the period between the change of teeth and puberty. The great thing is to enable the human being to find his place in the world with due confidence in his own power of judgment. He will then feel and sense his complete manhood because his education has been truly and completely human. If someone has been unfortunate enough to have lost a leg or an arm, he cannot feel himself a complete man; he is conscious of mutilation. Children of fourteen or fifteen, educated according to modern methods, begin to be aware of a sense of mutilation if they are not permeated with the qualities of moral judgment and religious feeling. Something seems lacking in their manhood. There is no better heritage in the moral and religious sense than to bring children up to regard the elements of morality and religion as such an integral part of their being, that they do not feel themselves wholly man if they are not permeated with morality, warmed through and through by religion.

This can only be achieved if we work, at the proper age, on the life of feeling and perceptive experience alone, and do not prematurely give the children intellectual conceptions of religion and morality. If we do so before the twelfth or fourteenth year, we are bringing children up to be sceptics—men and women who, instead of healthy insight, in later life develop scepticism in regard to the dogmas inculcated into them—to begin with, scepticism in thought (the least important), but then scepticism in feeling, which makes them defective in feeling. And finally there will be scepticism of will which brings moral error in its train. The point is this: our children will be brought up only to be sceptics if we present moral and religious ideals to them dogmatically; such ideals should only come to them through the life of feeling. Then, at the right age they will awaken their own free sense of religion and morality which will then become part of their very being. And they feel that only this can make them fully man. The great aim at the Waldorf School is to bring up free human beings who know how to direct their own lives.

. . . .

The Waldorf School is an organism complete and whole in itself, and if it is not thought of as such, many of its educational principles may be misunderstood. People may think for instance, that if they go to the School two or three times and see what is done on these particular days, that is sufficient; they have seen how we teach at the Waldorf School. That, of course, is not the case. They have seen nothing of any consequence. What they have seen is like a fragment cut out of a picture from which they then proceed to form an opinion of the whole. Suppose you take a fragment of some great picture and show it to someone. How can he form any opinion of the whole picture from this one fragment? The essential feature of Waldorf School education is that every activity has its place within the organism of the whole School. People will understand the Waldorf School much better by studying its principles, its whole structure, the organic connection between the eighth class and the fourth class, for instance, or between the first and the tenth, than by acquainting themselves with one isolated fragment of the teaching. The organization of the School is so conceived that each activity has its rightful place and time and fits in with the whole. And it is from this point of view that individual subjects of instruction are introduced into the School. Let me give an example by briefly describing in principle how eurhythmy is given its place in the whole work.

It is no good setting out to discover things which may then be introduced into the school activities. It is, as a rule, a wrong principle to think out certain things that are good for children—as has happened too frequently in the Froebel Kindergarten system—and then set them up as an essential part of education. Nothing should be artificially introduced into the school; it should all proceed from life itself. The teacher should have a free, unprejudiced outlook on life, an understanding of life, and be able to teach and educate children for life. The more intimately the teacher is connected with the life around, the better for the school. Narrow-minded teachers who know nothing of life except the school itself, can do little to develop the full manhood of a human being.—Eurhythmy was introduced into the Waldorf School not because we thought gymnastic exercises were necessary for the children and so set about inventing something. No, indeed! Eurhythmy did not arise, to begin with, as an educational measure at all. It arose as the result of certain connections of destiny, about the year 1912, but primarily as an art, not as an educational measure at all. And there will always be an imperfect idea of eurhythmy as applied in education if it is thought of as a special educational eurhythmy, distinct from eurhythmy as an art. For this reason, I myself should have thought it much better if the demonstrations of eurhythmy as an art had been given here first, for that would have shown the underlying conception. Because eurhythmy is in art, it is part of life and this part of life has been put into a form suitable for educational purposes. Nobody can understand eurhythmy as performed by children who does not realize what it will one day be as an art—and perhaps more than many people think, already is to-day.

Eurhythmy as an art came into being about the year 1912, but to begin with only as an art. The Waldorf School began in 1919 and because we have found that the art of eurhythmy can be applied in the education of children, we have introduced it into the School. That, however, is secondary. This connection should be realized in everything else if we would understand the Waldorf School in its relation to life. It is not a question of a special method of teaching children painting, for instance; if we want them to learn how to paint, the principles of the teaching should be drawn from the living art of painting and not from methods that have been specially put together for the purpose of education.

The element of real art must be introduced into schools, not an intellectual substitute for art. And with eurhythmy it is indeed possible again to infuse art into human culture.

In the addresses given before the performances, I have explained the sense in which eurhythmy is a visible speech— speech expressed in movement. I only want now to add something about these figures,* for this will still further

* Figures carved from wood and painted in different colours, characterizing the different movements and gestures of eurhythmy.

explain the relation of eurhythmy to art. The idea of the figures came, in the first place, from Miss Maryon but they have been carried out in the form which I think right and in strict accordance with the laws of eurhythmy.

Here (showing a figure), you have a picture of the sound S. The figure does in a sense represent a human being, but those who think in the sense of modern civilization and convention of what would be deemed a beautiful human form, will not find much beauty in the figure. They will see nothing of what strikes them as beautiful in a human being they meet in the street, perhaps. Now when it comes to making such figures, we may also have an eye for beauty of the human form, but the object in this case is to represent what comes to expression in eurhythmy, namely, the human being in movement. And so in these figures we have ignored everything that does not belong to the nature and form of the movement itself, the feeling corresponding to the particular movement, penetrating the basic character expressed by and colouring the movement. When you sing, you take into your whole organism—in a bodily sense—the elements that move the soul. The movement takes its course entirely within the limits of the skin and remains invisible, flowing wholly into the tone that is heard.

The figure you see here, expresses music in movement. What the soul feels, releases itself from the human being, becomes movement in space and the artistic element expresses itself in the form of the movement. We see what we otherwise hear. And so these figures are only intended to draw attention to what the human being becomes in doing eurhythmy, apart altogether from the attributes which nature imparts to him. Each movement is then indicated by the shape of the carving and the wood is painted with a certain fundamental colour. We have written at the back of the figures, the names of the colours corresponding to the movements themselves and to the feeling inherent in these movements. The way in which the eurhythmists on the stage manipulate their veils is really a continuation of the movement. When the eurhythmists have learnt to do this skilfully, the veil will float freely, be drawn back, caught up or given a definite form at the right moment. The movement carried out by the limbs underlies the feeling that is then expressed by the manipulation of the veil; the feeling comes to expression in the floating veil. If the eurhythmist has true feeling for the movement of arms or legs, the quality will instinctively pass over into the manipulation of the veil, the feeling which should accompany the movement in the handling of the veil will be felt.

Thirdly, when this movement (pointing to figure) is being made, the eurhythmist must be able to feel that the arm is stretching out lightly in this direction, as though it were hovering in the air without inner tension. In the other arm, she must feel as if she is summoning all her muscular force and packing it all tightly into the arm. One arm (the right) is held lightly upwards; the left arm is tense, and the muscles are almost throbbing. That is how the movement is given character, and this character in the movement makes an impression on the spectators. They feel what the eurhythmist is doing.

Now when the people look at these figures, they may ask, where is the face shown and where the back of the head. That, however, has nothing to do with eurhythmy. You will sometimes find people who are enthusiastic over the pretty face of a eurhythmist, but that, I assure you, is no part of eurhythmy! The face on this figure here, which seems as you look at it to be turned to the left, is really facing you, and the colour is used to emphasize that the eurhythmist should feel eurhythmic force lightly diffused over the right side of the head while the left side of the head is tense, penetrated by inner strength. It is as though the head becomes asymmetrical—relaxed, as if fluffed out on the one side, taut on the other.

In this way the movements receive their true character. These figures here express what ought to become visible in eurhythmy. The same principles hold good in all artistic work. One ought to be able to look away from the substance, the content, the prose, and enter into the artistic, poetic element. The beautiful face of a eurhythmist really corresponds to the prose quality. What she expresses when the right side of her head is lightly diffused with eurhythmic forces and the left side tense—that is what constitutes the real beauty in eurhythmy. So we can conceive that quite a plain face may be eurhythmically beautiful and a beautiful face ugly!

In eurhythmy, then, we have elements that hold good for every art—as all artists will agree. A great artist is not merely one who can paint a beautiful girl's face pleasingly. A true artist must, under certain conditions also be able to paint an old, wizened, wrinkled face in such a way that it becomes artistically beautiful. This must underlie all art.

I wanted to add these remarks about the eurhythmy you have seen in the performances here. Let me only say now that we have introduced eurhythmy into our Waldorf School because it affords such a wonderful contrast to ordinary gymnastics. As already indicated, bodily exercises are adequately carried out in the Waldorf School, but as regards ordinary, external gymnastics, we elaborate them in such a way that with every exercise the child is first given a sense of space, of the directions of space which are there, of course, as the primary thing. The child feels the direction of space and then his arms follow it. In his gymnastics he gives himself to space. This is the only healthy basis for gymnastic exercises. Space is conditioned in all directions. To our abstract conception of space, there are three directions which we can in no way distinguish. They are only there in geometry. In reality, however, the head is above, the legs below—there we have the above and below. Then we have right and left. We live in this direction of space when we stretch out our arms. The point is not to ask: where is the absolute direction? Of course we can turn this way or that. And then we have our forward and backward direction, front and behind. All other directions of space are oriented with respect to these. If we understand space in this way, we can discover really healthy movements for gymnastics, where the human being gives himself up, as it were, to the laws of space.

In the eurhythmy, the character of the movement is determined by the human organism, and then the question is: what is the soul experiencing in this movement or that? This indeed underlies the eurhythmic movements for the different sounds. What is happening when the forces of your being flow into the limbs? In the ordinary gymnastic exercises the human being lends himself to space; in eurhythmy he carries out movements that express his being and are in accordance with the laws of his organism. To allow what is inner to express itself outwardly in movement—that is the essence of eurhythmy. To fill the outer with the human being so that the human being unites himself with the outer world—that is the essence of gymnastics.

To educate the whole human being we can therefore derive gymnastics from the opposite pole to that of eurhythmy, where the movements come forth entirely from the inner being of man, but in any case, even where it is applied in education, the eurhythmic element itself must be derived from a true grasp of the artistic principles of eurhythmy.

My opinion is that the best teachers of gymnastics are those who have learnt from art. The impulses underlying the gymnastics of Greek schools and the Olympic games were derived from art. And if the consequences of what I have said are fully realized and all school work is based primarily upon the element of art, we shall apply what I have explained by the example of eurhythmy to other branches of life and activity as well. We shall not set out to invent something specifically for teaching, but rather to imbue the school with real life. And then from out of the school will grow life within the social order.

· · · · · · · ·

I have said that a school ought to be an organism in which each single feature is an integral part of the whole. The threads of the different activities which must be carried on in order that the whole organism of the Waldorf School may live, are drawn together in the very frequent teachers' meetings. In the course of the year, I myself am present at the majority of these meetings. They are not held merely for the purpose, should we say, of preparing school reports, conferring about administrative details or the punishments which are to be meted out to the children when they have broken rules and the like. These meetings are really the living "High School" for the College of Teachers—a permanent training academy, as it were. They are so indeed, and for the reason that every practical experience gained by the teacher in school becomes, in turn, part of his own education. And he who derives such self-education for himself from his teaching work, gaining on the one hand a profound psychological insight into the practical side of education and on the other into the different qualities, characters and temperaments of the children, will always be finding something new, for himself and for the whole College of Teachers. All the experience and knowledge acquired from the teaching should be "put into the pool" at these meetings. In this way the College of Teachers in spirit and soul becomes a whole where each member knows what the other is doing, what experience has taught him and what progress he has made as the result of his work with the children in the classroom. The College of Teachers becomes, in effect, a central organ whence the whole life-blood of the practical teaching flows and helps the teacher to maintain his freshness and vitality. Probably the best effect of all is that these meetings enable the teachers to maintain their inner vitality instead of actually growing old in soul and spirit. It must be the teacher's constant aim to maintain a youthful freshness of soul and spirit, but this can only be done if true life-blood flows to a central organ, just as human blood flows to the heart, and out of it again. That is concentrated as a system of soul-spiritual forces in the life that is striven for in the teachers' meetings at the Waldorf School. The meetings are held every week, and, as I said, from time to time in my presence.

And now I want to mention something that seems, on the face of it, trifling, but yet is important. As I told you, we have boys and girls together in the classes. It naturally happens that in some classes, girls are in the majority, in others, boys, and there are others in which the number of boys and girls is the same. A rationalist may visit these classes and give vent to all manner of intellectualistic opinions which, however, do not generally hit the nail on the head so far as actual life is concerned. If we are teaching in a class where girls are in the majority, things are not at all the same as in classes where the number of boys and girls is the same, or where boys are in the majority. The classes are not given their individual character by what the boys and girls do together, perhaps also the various silly things they do together, but by intangible elements that wholly escape outer, intellectualistic observation. Highly interesting things come to light when we study this intangible life of the class. Naturally the teacher must not come into the room and stepping back with folded arms proceed to "study" the pupils! If the teacher brings sufficient vitality and devotion to the work with his pupils, then simply by taking them with him through sleep, as it were, in the right way, he will wake up next morning with really significant discoveries about the happenings in school on the previous day; he will become aware of this process in a comparatively short time, and everything that should happen in this way will do so as a matter of course.

Just as at the centre of school life the teachers' meetings are essential, so at the periphery the parents' evenings we have at the Waldorf School are of the very greatest importance. At least once a month, at any rate periodically, we try to arrange evenings when the parents of the children at the school come together, if they can, to meet the teachers in order that a link may be made with the children's home life. We set great store by this understanding for the child's school life on the part of the parents. Since we do not draw up programmes and schedules for our teaching, but draw it from life itself, we cannot adopt the attitude which says: "I have done the right thing because I have carried out the time-table laid down by an intelligent authority." We must learn to feel what is the right thing to do in living intercourse with those who as parents, as those responsible, have sent their children to us in the school. And the echoes that reach the teachers when we have these parents' evenings, bring life to what the teachers especially need to maintain their own inner vitality.

A living being does not live simply within its skin; nor is man merely a being who stands in the space inside his skin. At every moment we have a certain volume of air within ourselves. Before we breathed this air into our lungs, it was outside, it belonged to the whole atmosphere. Very soon it will again be breathed out into the atmosphere. A living being belongs to the whole universe, is a member or limb of the universe; existence is unthinkable apart from the universe. And so it is with man's life and being. Man is not an isolated entity within the social order but an integral member of it. He cannot live unless he is related to the outer social order as closely as his physical organism enclosed by his skin is related to air and water. It needs very little to show how much depends upon the school in this connection.—I always try to take examples to illustrate these things from near at hand, not from something thought-out, and two days ago I went into a room in this building and saw a report from the Sunday School teachers. The very first sentence refers to the words of one of the chairmen—a very eminent man—at the yearly meeting of the Sunday School Union. He said that these Sunday Schools had gradually developed an exclusiveness, a remoteness from other religious life in the world—that there was in fact, too little knowledge of religious life in general. I read this on the notice-board in the room next door, and it is a vital symptom of what is needed for the inner vitalization of civilization to-day. I might quite well find the same kind of thing on another board or have some leaflet given me in the street; everything tells the same story which is, that men and women to-day are not brought up with a wide horizon in life, a full understanding of life. This quality is essential to the Waldorf School teachers and it must be communicated by them to their pupils, so that education and teaching may lead to wide interests in life. Everyone is so shut in, so confined, to-day! Think how training for a profession is conducted. It results in people being almost ashamed of knowing anything outside the pigeon-hole of their profession. One is always told to go to the expert or specialist! The great essential is for men and women to be wide-hearted, to be able to participate with their hearts and souls in culture and civilization as a whole. This is what we try, through the principles of education, first to inculcate into the teachers—for in the Waldorf School the primary thing has been to educate them—and then through the teachers, into the pupils. And the pupils are our great hope, our goal, for our constant thought in every measure adopted is that they shall bear its fruits into life in the right way.

That, my dear friends, is the attitude underlying the art of education of which I have been speaking to you. It is based wholly on this principle; the measures adopted in education and teaching must be derived from the very being of man, so that on the one hand he shall develop full manhood in body, soul and spirit, and on the other that he shall find his place in life, having in childhood—again in body, soul and spirit—grown up in a religious, ethical, artistic and intellectual life and so have been enabled to develop virtues best fitted to be of use to his fellow-men. Fundamentally speaking, every ideal of education must be based on this principle, and I am indeed grateful to those who made it possible for me to speak here on the subject.

I am sure you will have realized that although the principles of Waldorf School education were born in one particular country, there is no question of any element of nationalism, but rather of internationalism in the best sense, because the issue is that of the universal human. Our aim is to educate human beings with wide, rich interests—not men and women who belong to a particular class, nation or professional category. And so I think you will agree that, although this art of education emanates from a particular country, it is permissible to speak of it in other lands too.

Greater still is my pleasure to find that in connection with what has been said in these lectures, a Committee has been formed, to establish a school and so bring the Waldorf School principles of education into this country in a really practical way.* When it is a question of founding such schools to-day, the only thing we can do is to make model, pattern schools as it were—and that applies to the Waldorf School as well. For not until the principles underlying this art of education are acknowledged by the widest circles of public opinion, can their impulse be really fruitful.

I remember in my early youth that I once saw in a comic paper, a joke about architects' plans.—I mentioned something of the sort yesterday.—The paper, wishing to address people of somewhat limited intelligence, because its circulation was among this class, said that one should not go to an architect who would make all kinds of drawings and calculations about details and set to work to put the materials together artistically, but rather to an ordinary mason, who just lays one brick on another.—Now this attitude still largely dominates the educational world. People are very prone to regard the architect's work as abstract and they would like to see brick laid upon brick without bothering with the principle that must underlie the whole structure. Be that as it may, I am sincerely grateful to find such splendid understanding and interest among you who have come to these lectures. First, let me thank Miss Beverley and her helpers, then our Waldorf School teachers and other friends who have worked so well and with such deep understanding, and also those who have added the artistic element to our Conference. I am grateful indeed to all whose interest and sincerity have brought into being a Conference which I hope will bear fruit through the newly formed Committee. The more this interest spreads, the more we shall be able to serve the true principles of education. That you have this at heart has been proved by your living co-operation, and so I should like to close these lectures—which I have not given from the intellect alone but from profound interest in the principles of true education—with a parting greeting to you all.

* The New School, Streatham, London, now Michael Hall, Forest Row, Sussex.

SPECIAL LECTURE

Three Epochs in the Religious Education of Man

The week-day lectures of this course are devoted to the special subject of education. This Sunday lecture will be different in character and content. From the education of the child on Earth—from the human art of education we are seeking to develop—we will look upward to the Divine educators of mankind as a whole. They, the great cosmic educators, have led mankind from age to age of history and evolution, through a diversity of religious and ethical aspirations, related to the different stages in man's knowledge of the world around him. For if we look at history as one great whole, we see it—in spite of the many valleys and lowlands breaking the heights of the ascending development of man—as a continuous education of the human race, as a process whereby a religious, a divine consciousness penetrates ever and again into mankind.

In every epoch of human evolution there has existed some kind of Initiation Science, analogous, in its own way, to the Initiation Science outlined in my book *Knowledge of the Higher Worlds and its Attainment*. What I have there described is the Initiation Science of the present age, and it leads from a mere knowledge of Nature to a knowledge of the Spirit.

To this Initiation Science the course of human evolution is revealed in a threefold light. We can look back to a very ancient epoch which came to a close about the eighth century B.C. Then we see an epoch radiant in the light of the Mystery of Golgotha, when through Christ Jesus an everlasting impulse entered into human evolution; and so too, there can arise in our vision a third epoch, at the beginning of which we stand to-day and which we have to bring to a deeper reality by means of a new Initiation Science.

Now over and above what is imparted to man by his natural intelligence, reason, will and feeling and by his earthly education, each of these three epochs has striven for something else. In each of these epochs man has sensed the existence of a mighty riddle, deeply interwoven with his destiny. And always this riddle has assumed a different form because the human race has passed through different conditions of soul in the several epochs. It is only in the modern age of abstractions that the human soul is imagined to have remained more or less unchanged ever since man evolved, as is mistakenly supposed, out of the animal kingdom.

Those whom a deeper science has enabled to gaze with unbiassed vision into the reality of life, realize that the constitution of the human soul in the first epoch of evolution was not by any means the same as in the epoch crowned by the Mystery of Golgotha. Again there is a difference in our own times, when we must seek to understand this Mystery of Golgotha anew if we are not to lose it as a fact of knowledge.

In this sense, then, let us consider the nature of the human soul in the ancient East, in an age which produced the wisdom contained in the Vedas and the Vedanta philosophy. Everywhere to-day men are turning back, often with great misunderstanding, to the Vedas and the Vedanta. If we look at the souls of men in the ancient East, even at souls living in the old Chaldean-Assyrian-Babylonian civilization and in the earliest Greek period, we find that they were of quite a different nature from the souls of men living to-day. The souls of men in those ancient times lived in a more dreamlike, spiritual existence than the souls of modern men, who in their waking life are wholly given up to sense impressions, to all that the intellect can derive from these sense impressions and to the memory of them. What really constitutes the substance of the soul of man to-day, did not bear the same form in the souls of the ancients. These men possessed a much more instinctive wisdom of the inner life of soul and spirit. What we to-day would speak of as the faculty of clear and conscious discernment, did not as yet exist. Man experienced a weaving, moving inner life, the shadowy echoes of which remain in our present dream-life. It was an *inner* life, in which man not only knew with certainty that a soul was weaving and moving through his body, forming part of his true manhood, but in which he also knew: A soul, born from a divine-spiritual existence before a body clothed me in my earthly form, is living within me.

In those ancient times man experienced his own being in a kind of waking dream. He knew himself *as a soul*, and in this living inner experience he felt the body as a kind of sheath, merely an instrument for the purposes of earthly life. Even in his waking hours man lived in this consciousness of soul—dreamlike though it was. And he knew with clear conviction that before a physical body clothed him on Earth, he had lived as soul in a divine-spiritual world. Direct inner perception revealed to him this life of soul and spirit, and, as a consequence, his consciousness of death was quite different from that of modern man. To-day man feels that he is deeply linked with his body. His inner consciousness of soul is not detached from his bodily life as was the case in earlier times. He looks upon birth as a beginning, death as an end.

So living and intimate was the experience of the permanent, eternal nature of the soul in the ancients, that they felt themselves raised above birth and death in their contemplation of this life of soul. Birth and death were states of growth, metamorphoses of life. They knew the reality of a pre-earthly existence, and hence with equal certainty they knew that they would live beyond the gate of death. Birth and death were transitory occurrences in an unceasing life.

It has, however, always been necessary for man's immediate experience to be widened and deepened by a knowledge that penetrates to the spiritual world, by an Initiation Science that tells him more than can arise within his inner being or is imparted to him by earthly education in his ordinary life. It fell to the old Initiates, the teachers of that ancient humanity, to give the answer to a definite riddle that arose in the souls of men. As I have said, the men of that time knew of the soul and spirit by immediate experience. Yet for them too there was a great riddle, and it arose in the soul in this form: Through conception and birth I pass into physical life and move upon earth; I am clothed in a physical body, containing the very same substances as those of dead, outer Nature. Thus I am clothed in something that is foreign to my inmost being. Between birth and death I live in a body—a body of outer Nature. I am born in a physical sense but this physical birth is foreign to my inner being.

The mighty riddle before the man of very ancient times, as he gazed into his innermost being, was not a riddle connected with the soul and spirit, but with *Nature*. And it arose before him as he sensed the full inner reality of soul and spirit, and then felt the need to understand why he was clothed in a physical body so foreign to his real being. It was the task of Initiation Science to teach man how he could direct the same forces which enabled him to gaze into the life of soul and spirit, to outer Nature as well—to Nature whose manifestations are otherwise dumb and inarticulate. And if after adequate training—so it was taught by that ancient Initiation Science—man directs to stone and plant and animal, to clouds and stars, to the courses of Sun and Moon, the forces which otherwise lead only to an inner knowledge of the soul, he can know and understand outer Nature as well. Then he beholds the Spiritual not only in his inner being but also in bubbling spring, flowing river and mountain, in the gathering clouds, in lightning and thunder, in stone and plant and animal.

Thus did an ancient Initiation Science speak to man: "Gazing into thine own being, thou hast a living experience of soul and spirit, thou findest the Divine within thee. Initiation Science will now train the power which otherwise beholds the Divine in man alone, also to behold the Divine in the whole life of Nature. Thou art clothed in an outer physical body. Know that this body too is from God. Physical birth has brought thee into an earthly existence which is itself of Divine origin."

And so the task of ancient Initiation Science was to give man this sublime teaching: "Know that thou are born of God not only when thine eyes gaze inward. In the body that comes into the world through physical birth—there also thou are born of God." All that the old Father Initiation placed before the soul of man was expressed in after times, in three penetrating words:

Ex Deo Nascimur.

This was the first way in which Initiation Wisdom worked upon man and awakened a religious consciousness within him. The old heathen cults assumed the form of Nature-religions because man felt the need for a justification of his physical birth in Nature. Nature was the riddle to his soul; in the *Ex Deo nascimur* the riddle of Nature was solved and he could feel his earthly existence hallowed, though in his waking life he still felt himself a being of spirit and soul, transcending the physical.

· · · · · · · ·

As the course of evolution continued, man's early, dream-like experience of soul and spirit—which was indeed a kind of innate knowledge of his true inner being—faded gradually into the background. He began more and more to use the instruments afforded by his physical body. Let me express it as follows: The dreams of a life of soul and spirit that characterized a primal instinct in the human race, faded away into darkness, and for the first time, in the last thousand years before the Mystery of Golgotha, men learnt to make use of their outer senses and of the intellect bound up with these outer senses. What we to-day call "Nature" now first appeared before men as an actual experience. It had been the task of the old wise Initiates to explain the spirituality of Nature to the human soul. The purely *physical* quality of outer Nature was now there as a question before the soul. To the old riddle of man's earthly existence there was added the second great riddle in the history of evolution—that of man's *earthly death.*

It was only in the last thousand years before the Mystery of Golgotha that man came to feel death upon Earth with any real intensity. Whereas in earlier times he had little sense of his body and a strong sense of soul and spirit, he now felt and experienced his life in the physical body. Death, the enigmatic event that is bound up with the physical body, was experienced by him as the greatest riddle of existence in this second epoch. The riddle of death emerges with great intensity among the ancient Egyptians, for instance. They embalmed their corpses because they experienced the terror of death, because they were aware of the kinship of the physical body (in which they sensed their own existence) with death. "How do I live in my earthly body?" had been the first riddle. "How do I pass through earthly death?" was the second.

In the days when man had gazed upward to the soul and spirit, when the soul and spirit were immediate experience to his instinctive clairvoyance, he knew: When the chains that bind me to this earthly existence fall away, I shall belong to the Earth no more. My earthly being will be changed, and lo! I shall once again be living in the realms beyond the Earth, I shall be united with the stars.—For the soul knew the stars *spiritually* in the instinctive life of olden time. Man read his destiny in the stars. He felt himself united with Sun and Moon; he knew the stars. "From the Spirit in the stars, from a pre-earthly existence I have come forth. To the stars—to the Spirit in the stars—I shall return when I pass through the gate of death."

But now all this became a riddle. Man confronted death, beholding in death the body's end. He felt his soul inwardly bound to the body, and with a deep awareness of this riddle he asked himself: "What becomes of me after death? How do I pass through the portal of death?" And to begin with, there was nothing on the Earth which could help him solve the riddle.

The old Initiates knew how to explain to man the riddle of Nature. *Ex Deo nascimur*—this was how they answered, if we translate their words into a later tongue. But now, all consciousness of the pre-earthly existence whither man would return after he had passed the gate of death, all that had been so clear in former times, was obliterated from the human soul. The instinctive knowledge arising in man inasmuch as his own life of soul and spirit reached upward to the stars, was no longer there. And then a mighty event occurred. The Spirit of the world of stars—He whom a later age called "Christ", and an earlier Greek age, the "Logos"—descended upon Earth, descended in His Substance as a Spiritual Being and took flesh upon Himself in the human body of Jesus of Nazareth. It was given to mankind to experience the greatest event of all earthly existence. He whose life had been divined by the ancients as they gazed upward to the stars, the Godhead of whom the Divine-Earthly is also part, passed through earthly life and death. For the death and resurrection of Christ were the most essential thing for those early Christians who truly understood Christianity.

And so, this passing of the God who in earlier times had only revealed Himself from the stars—this passing of the Godhead through a human body—contained the solution of the second riddle of existence, the riddle of death, inasmuch as the mystery was revealed in the so-called Gnosis by the Initiates of the age of the Mystery of Golgotha. The Initiates could now teach men: The Being who dwelt erstwhile in Eternity amid the stars, has descended into a human body and has vanquished death in a human body. The Christ has now become an "extract" of the Spirit—or of the Logos—of the Universe. The old Initiates had pointed to Nature, saying: "Out of God is this Nature born." Now the Initiates could teach man how he can be united with the Divine Being who descended into Jesus of Nazareth, who in the man Jesus of Nazareth passed, as all men pass, through the gate of death, but who then conquered death. And once again it was possible for man to solve this second riddle—the riddle of Death—even as he had formerly solved the riddle of Nature.

In Buddhism we are told that the Buddha found the four great Truths, one of which awoke within him at the sight of a corpse, when he was seized by the utter desolation of the human body in death. About six hundred years *before* the

Mystery of Golgotha, as a last remnant of ancient thought, Buddha had the vision of death. Six hundred years *after* the Mystery of Golgotha, men began to gaze at the dead human form on the Cross. And just as Buddha believed that in the corpse he had discovered the great truth of suffering, as a last fragment of ancient wisdom, so now a humanity permeated with the Christ impulse gazed at the dead figure on the Cross, at the crucifix, and felt in this figure the heavenly guarantee of a life beyond death—for death had been conquered by Christ in the body of Jesus.

Because of their fear of death, the Egyptians embalmed their corpses, to preserve, as it were, the Nature-forces in man from death. This was in the age of *Ex Deo nascimur*. The early Christians, in whom the impulse of esoteric Christianity was still living, buried their dead, holding divine service over the grave in the sure conviction that death is conquered by the soul that is united with Christ; the tomb became an altar. From the Mystery of Golgotha flowed the certainty that if man is united with Christ, who as the spiritual essence of the stars descended upon Earth and passed through life and death and resurrection in a human form, he himself as man will also conquer death.

Thus *God the Father* was the answer to the riddle of Nature. *Christ* was the answer to the riddle of death. Death had lost its sting. By a more powerful argument than had formerly been necessary, death now became the metamorphosis of life.

The Gnosis—which was later exterminated, and of which fragments only have been preserved—proves that as the Christian Initiates contemplated the Mystery of Golgotha, in the certainty that Christ had descended to Earth and had awakened to new life the death-bringing forces in the Earth, they were able to instil into humanity the truth of the union of mortal man on Earth with Christ. Through Christ, man redeems the forces of death within him and awakens them to *life*. Thus the Initiates were now able to impart a new consciousness of immortality to men, saying: "Your souls can be united with Him who passed through the Mystery of

Golgotha; you too can live in the life and death and resurrection of Christ. If your earthly life is more than a mere natural existence, if it is such that Christ's Kingdom is awakened in your dealings with all your fellow-men, then are you living in communion with Christ Himself. Christ, the Divine Being, becomes your brother; in death and in life you die in Christ." The truth of life in God the Son, in Christ, could now be added to the primeval truth of birth from God the Father, and to *Ex Deo nascimur* was added:

In Christo Morimur.

"In Christ we die"—that is to say—"as a soul, we live!"

Such was the wisdom of man in the epoch that began about a thousand years before the Mystery of Golgotha and came to its close in the fifteenth century A.D. And we are now living in a third epoch which we must learn to understand aright. So in the education of the human race, directed by the great Divine Teachers of the world, there was added to the truth "Out of God the Father we are born" this truth—"In Christ the Son we die, to the end that we may live."

. . . .

The great riddles of the first and second epochs stand before us clearly when we look back over ancient history. The riddle of the third epoch in which we have been living for some centuries is as yet little known or felt, though it is there subconsciously in the feeling life of man and he yearns for its solution as deeply as he once yearned for the solution of the riddle of his earthly nature and then of his earthly death.

Since the fourteenth and fifteenth centuries man has acquired a knowledge that penetrates deeply into Nature. Think only of the starry heavens which were once revealed to the dream-consciousness of the ancients and from which they read their destiny. External calculations, geometry and mechanics have taught man more and more about the stars since the approach of our present age. The science of the stars and of animals and plants has spread abroad in the form of a purely natural science. It was very different in the first epoch of human evolution and different again in the second, when in the depths of their souls men knew the truth of the Divine reality which the old clairvoyant powers of the soul read in the stars, and which in Christ descended into the body of Jesus of Nazareth. Christ was alive among men. The men of the second epoch looked to the Christ, they felt Him in their hearts, and in this deep communion with Him they experienced what the Spirit of the Cosmos had once revealed to an old dreamlike clairvoyant consciousness, giving justification and meaning to this earthly life. In the second epoch, man lived, as it were, in the cosmic spheres, inasmuch as he lived in communion with the Christ who had descended from these cosmic spheres to Earth.

Then came the third epoch, when the world of stars was understood merely through calculation, when men looked through the telescope and spectroscope and discovered in the stars the same dead elements and substances as exist on the Earth. In this epoch men can no longer see Christ as the Being who descended from the stars, because they do not know that the stars themselves are the expression of the Spiritual Essence weaving through the Cosmos. And so the Cosmos is void of God, bereft of Christ, for mankind to-day.

Therefore it is that the inner consciousness of man is now menaced by the danger of losing Christ. The first signs are already visible. The ideas of Divine Wisdom or Theology, which for centuries contained a knowledge of the Christ-revelation, are now in many respects powerless to find the Christ, the God in the man Jesus of Nazareth. Many who contemplate the age of the Mystery of Golgotha no longer find Christ as a Cosmic Being; they find only the man—Jesus of Nazareth. The starry heavens are bereft of God, they are a mere part of Nature, and men can no longer recognize in Him who passed through the Mystery of Golgotha, the Being whose physical kingdom is the entire Cosmos, yet who also entered into the man Jesus of Nazareth during the Mystery of Golgotha.

Inasmuch as these things are deeply experienced in his

inner being, there is a difference between one who treads the path of modern Initiation Wisdom and one who merely learns external Natural Science. This Natural Science has lost the Spirit of the Cosmos, and the danger is drawing near that humanity will also lose the Christ, even in Jesus of Nazareth.

Therefore it is that those who in our age penetrate more deeply into the knowledge of Nature that has blossomed forth in the third period of human evolution—since the fourteenth or fifteenth centuries—feel the third great riddle of man's earthly development. They look back in history to the first great riddle—that of man's earthly nature; to the second riddle, that of his earthly death. And the third riddle arises within them, whispering something which as yet men do not like to face, although they feel it subconsciously and with a certain emphasis in their hearts. The Initiates of our age say to themselves: "We are living in the world which once spoke to man from out of the Cosmos,—spoke as the *Spirit*. In days of yore man lived a life of full wakefulness in the Cosmos. Gradually this waking life in the Cosmos, also this feeling of oneness with the Christ who descended to Earth to preserve this awareness of the spiritual Cosmos in man, faded away, and we are now living in a Cosmos that is revealed to us merely in its outer aspect. Modern cosmology is experienced as a kind of dream. The Cosmos is weighed in the scales of a balance, observed by the telescope. Such is our dream! And instead of uniting us with the Spirit of the Cosmos, this dream has separated us from Him."

And so the third great riddle of the *sleep of knowledge*, the sleep into which mankind has fallen, stands before those who live in the third epoch of evolution, the third epoch, not only of "uninitiated" but of Initiation Science.

The deepest thinkers of the human race have felt this. Descartes felt it, for he finally began to doubt the validity of all knowledge yielded by outer Nature. But, to begin with, it was felt only dimly. More and more deeply there must enter into men the consciousness that the whole domain of knowledge of which they have been so proud for some five centuries, represents a sleep of existence. This third great riddle must stand more and more clearly before them. In former times men asked themselves: Why do we have to dwell in an earthly, physical body ? Why do we pass through earthly death ? In the third epoch this question arises in the hearts of men: Why this *sleep* of a knowledge directed merely to outer Nature ? How can we awaken from the dream that this "calculated" universe represents, how can we pass from this Cosmos whose external aspect is revealed through Astro-Physics and Astro-Chemistry, and stand face to face with the Cosmos that in the depths of our innermost being unites us once again with its deepest Essence ? How can we awaken from the dream into which knowledge has fallen in recent times ?

Ex Deo nascimur—this was the answer given by the Initiates in the earliest times to man's question, "Why do I live in an earthly body ?" In the age of the Mystery of Golgotha the Initiates sought to solve the riddle of death by linking man with Christ Jesus who had passed through the Mystery of Golgotha, answering, in the words of a later tongue, *In Christo morimur*. And it is the task of modern Initiation Science, in this our age and in the following centuries, gradually to lead mankind to a divine consciousness, to a religious life, and make it possible for him to awaken in his innermost being a spiritual knowledge of the Cosmos. The Initiation Science that must arise through Anthroposophia does not wish merely to be an extension of our present sleeping knowledge—although men are proud of this knowledge and its outer successes have been so splendid. Anthroposophical Initiation Science would awaken this sleeping knowledge, would awaken man, who is fettered in the "dreams" of reason and intellectuality.

Hence, the Initiation Science that would be borne by Anthroposophia is not a mere extension of facts and discoveries of knowledge, but an impulse to an *awakening*, an attempt to answer the question: How can we awaken from the sleep of life ? And so, just as the earliest Initiates had explained *Ex Deo nascimur*, and those who came later *In Christo morimur*, the Initiation Wisdom which bears within itself a future life of conscious spiritual knowledge, a life leading to a deepening of religious feeling, to a divine consciousness—this Initition Wisdom would lead man once again to know that the Christ who passed through the Mystery of Golgotha is the Logos, weaving and working through the Cosmos. And inasmuch as man will gradually grow to be conscious of his cosmic existence, the Initiation Science that is intended to inaugurate a spiritual Christology in the truest sense (as well as an Art of Education, for instance, in a narrower sphere), will strive to bring a religious mood into the practical life it ever seeks to serve.—"Out of God we are born as physical human beings"—"In Christ we die"—that is to say, "as a soul, we live".—To these truths Initiation Science will ever strive to add the third: "*When we press forward through the new Initiation to the Spirit, then even in this earthly life we become alive in the Spirit.*" We experience an awakening of knowledge whereby all our life is bathed in the light of true religion, and in the light of a moral goodness proceeding from inner piety. In short, this new Initiation Science endeavours to supplement the answers to the first and second riddles of Initiation as expressed in the *Ex Deo nascimur* and in the *In Christo morimur*, while at the same time it solves them anew and restores them to the soul of man. It endeavours to bring afresh and in full clarity to the human heart, this other truth—a truth that will awaken the Spirit in man's heart and soul: In the understanding of the living Spirit, we ourselves, in body, soul and Spirit, shall be re-awakened—

Per Spiritum Sanctum Reviviscimus

Farewell Address

I have already expressed my gratitude to the Committee, Miss Beverley, and to all of you who have devoted this fortnight to the study of our subject, and you may be sure that a very warm sense of thankfulness will remain with me as a pleasant memory of this course of lectures.

I only want now to add a few words to what I have been describing in the lectures from many different points of view. Most of you are well aware of the connection between the educational principles of the Waldorf School Movement and what as Anthroposophy goes through the Anthroposophical Movement, and perhaps at the close of this Conference I may be permitted to say a few words on this subject.

The world to-day still has a mistaken opinion of the Anthroposophical Movement, and perhaps this is partly due to the fact that a certain wish of mine—however impracticable it may be—cannot be fulfilled. Although it is true that the Waldorf School Movement has grown out of the Anthroposophical Movement, it is is no less the fact that what I should prefer would be to give a different name to the Anthroposophical Movement every week! I realize what dreadful confusion that would create, but none the less it is what I should like best of all, for in our age names really do terrible harm. It is, of course, obvious what confusion there would be in people's minds if the letter-heads were changed every week, and if they got a letter printed with the previous week's name of the Society—since superseded! Nevertheless it would be an exceedingly good thing for the Anthroposophical Movement if we had no permanent name, for a large section of mankind to-day merely concern themselves with the name and do not penetrate into the subject itself.

People, one can find, turn to a Greek Lexicon and in their

particular tongue invent some form of words to express "Anthroposophy". They then proceed to create their own brand of Anthroposophy, and according to it we ourselves are judged in the world. People form an opinion about us according to the conception they have formed of the name, thinking that they can spare themselves from entering into the substance and essence of Anthroposophy.

The book-table at the door of this Hall has already disappeared, but I assure you that I shuddered every day as I came in and saw the mass of literature upon it! I should be glad if there were less; but, of course, people must study Anthroposophy—there is that about it! One cannot approach a mere name, and that is why it would be such a good thing if we were spared from the necessity of using any. That obviously would not do, but I think that in a course like this, dealing with a sphere of practical life, a practical application of Anthroposophy proves how remote our endeavours are from any sectarianism or wish to hurl dogmas at the heads of men and women, and that the only aim of Anthroposophy is to acquire knowledge of the world's realities in their very essence. If it is a question of taking any share in world-evolution, it is essential to have true insight into the course taken by events in the world.

It is a sad thing that in our time there is so little inclination to look into the course of world-happenings, and that is really the true task of Anthroposophy. That, too, is why we can speak of special domains like education, for instance, without taking our start from points on a scheduled programme or the like.

In founding the Waldorf School, we realized that it was not a question of introducing the rigid dogmatism which Anthroposophy is believed to represent, but far rather to introduce nothing of Anthroposophy as given for grown-up people. We realized that Anthroposophy must live in us as the power generating an unbiassed understanding of man's being and an unprejudiced observation of the world, leading thence to free action.

A short time ago I read an extraordinary criticism—it

was very antagonistic. There are many such, and I have no wish to speak of them in detail. This particular criticism says that I apparently make efforts to be unbiassed—but the words imply a grave rebuke! I should have thought it was a common duty in our age, especially in spiritual matters, to strive for open-minded knowledge, but apparently it can be a matter for severe reproach! However that may be, I think that particularly the subject of education may give rise to ready understanding between the Continent and England, and when I see what your attitude has been to these lectures, I cannot but regard it as an extraordinarily good symptom. In trying to describe our age, people so readily let slip the abstract phrase: "We are living in an age of transition." Now every age is an age of transition—from the preceding to the subsequent period. The point is—what it is that is in transition. At the present time all kinds of different symptoms show us that we are indeed caught up in the process of a mighty transition.

Perhaps I can describe it best by leading your thoughts back for a few minutes to the stage of spiritual evolution reached in England in the twelfth and thirteenth and beginning of the fourteenth centuries. At the beginning of the fourteenth century, everyone who claimed to be recognized as a person of culture spoke the French language. The English language consisted of dialects which did not find their way into the general culture of the people, and the language of science was Latin. If, for instance, we want to study the general nature of education in England in the fourteenth century, round about the year 1364, we can do so from Hykte's *Polychronicon*, which appeared at that time; the book is written in Latin, and makes it quite evident that the medium of culture in this country was the Latin tongue. Now while this book was being written—while, therefore, the language of culture was Latin—schools were gradually coming into being where the national language—and it was the same in other parts of Europe—began to find its way into education. Schools were founded in Winchester and in Oxford, where already the national tongue was used. In the second half of the fourteenth century we find the highly significant transition from the use of Latin—which is an international tongue—to the national tongue.

Similar transitions occur sooner or later in other regions of the civilized world, and this is a phenomenon of great significance. So far as England is concerned, we can place it in the second half of the fourteenth century. For when Hykte wrote his book in 1364, he was still able to tell us that the Latin tongue was the universal medium for education. When a certain Treviso translated the book into English in the year 1385, he tells us that the English language had been introduced into schools. Here, then, we see the transition from the international Latin tongue, in which people all over the world of culture discussed matters of education, to the age when the national tongue rises above the level of dialect to become, within the several peoples, a medium for education and teaching. And that is a most significant transition.

According to the anthroposophical view of the world, we can describe it as the transition from the age of the Intellectual Soul to that of the Spiritual Soul; for the essence of modern civilization is that a transition has taken place from the age of the Intellectual Soul, when man still feels himself more a member of the universe, to that of the Spiritual Soul, when he is to become conscious of his freedom, his inner power of resolve and action. And thus alone could the great world-process, in the midst of which we are still standing to-day, be instituted.

The effects produced by the emergence of the national tongue did not immediately penetrate into the souls and hearts of men, but to begin with, here in England too, the Renaissance movement, the so-called Humanist movement, began to flow from the South towards the North. In its early days, this Humanist movement indeed aspired towards the qualities of the Spiritual Soul, but did not come to the point of real understanding, and so it was established, that in order to be truly man one must absorb this humanist-classical culture. Up to our own day the centuries have been engaged in this struggle for human freedom, for the exercise of inner, spiritual activity. But more and more the needs of civilized humanity become apparent. In the age preceding the urge towards the Spiritual Soul, a language itself gave rise to the element of internationalism, making it possible for the cultured men of all countries to come to terms with one another. Language was the international element. This language—and we can place the actual transition in the second half of the fourteenth century—could not longer be the medium of international understanding. The urge within man was to unfold his spiritual activity from the depths of his own inner being. He resorted to the national tongue, and this made it more and more necessary that the understanding should come about at a level higher than that of language or speech.

We need a spirituality no longer proceeding merely from language, but issuing from the soul in a much more direct way. A true realization of Anthroposophy in historical connection with the present time shows us that its task is to find, all the world over, an international medium of understanding—one by means of which men can find their way to one another and which transcends the level of language and speech.

All that plays between man and man is incorporated by the faculty of speech into sounds communicated by the air. In speech, our being is really active in the material world. If we understand one another at a level higher than speech by means of deeper elements in the soul—by means of thoughts carried by feeling, warmed by the heart—then we have an international medium of understanding, but we need a heart for this for it to come into being. We must find the path to the spirit of man at a level higher than that of speech. The search for a language of thought, as well as all other matters connected with philosophy, education, religion, and art—that is the signification of the Anthroposophical Movement in the historical present.

Everyday speech lives and moves in the medium of air, has its existence still in the material world. The language striven for by Anthroposophy will move in the pure element of light that passes from soul to soul, from heart to heart—and this is more than a figure of speech. Modern civilization will need such a medium of understanding—not only for the things of higher culture, but also for the things of everyday life. Before this is realized, of course, many congresses having other points of view will be held, but of recent times the fruitfulness of such congresses for the healing of mankind has not been very apparent. The Anthroposophical Movement would intercede for a true healing of mankind that can only proceed from mutual understanding. And because this is so, we try to understand our own age in history, in order again to become man in the true sense—a humanity with a fully conscious soul, as was the case once, in another stage of evolution, when the Latin tongue was the medium of international understanding. The function once played by the Latin tongue must now be played by universal-human ideas, through which man may find his way to his fellowmen all over the earth.

In outer practical life, a body has already been created in world-economy, but this body as yet is without soul and spirit. Anything that lives in the world requires soul and spirit as well as a body. In the very truest sense, Anthroposophy would be the soul and spirit of the body that has come into being over the whole of civilization in world-economy and the other activities of practical life. Anthroposophy does not disdain to concern itself with the most practical branches of life; it would fain infuse them with the element that alone can conduce to the real progress of human evolution.

I am so infinitely grateful for your wish to understand how, in this sense, an attempt in the domain of education bases itself on the Anthroposophical Movement as representing a true conception of the present age in evolution; and I am grateful, too, for the interest you have shown in the lights and shades which I have tried to introduce into these lectures, in addition to speaking of the historical significance of the aims of this art of education. Expecially do I thank you for your cordial feelings towards a course of lectures given with the object of describing what Waldorf School education seeks to achieve for the progress of civilization in face of the needs of the present time.

I have tried to picture Waldorf School education as something that points to the deepest needs of mankind in the present age, and, as I say, your sympathetic understanding will indeed remain in my heart and soul as a very good memory of this course of lectures.

Steinerbooks

The Spiritual Sciences in paperback format, 5½" x 8¼" (unless otherwise noted).

ISBN Prefix: 0-89345

235-1	**Alchemists Through the Ages** (320 pp. illus.)	Waite
226-2	**Atlantis: The Antediluvian World** (512 pp. illus.)	Donnelly
246-7	**Beekeeping** (104 pp. illus.)	Steiner
201-7	**Christianity and Occult Mysteries of Antiquity** (256 pp.)	Steiner
227-0	**Cosmic Memory:** Atlantis and Lemuria (272 pp.)	Steiner
239-4	**Count of St. Germain** (260 pp.)	Cooper-Oakley
202-5	**Education As An Art** (128 pp.)	Steiner
203-3	**Fairy Tale of The Green Snake** (72 pp.)	Goethe & Steiner
223-8	**Gardening For Health:** The Bio-Dynamic Way (96 pp. illus.)	Philbrick
205-X	**Graphology:** The Science of Handwriting (128 pp. illus.)	Frith
228-9	**Great Initiates:** Secret History of Religions (528 pp.)	Schure
218-1	**Great Pyramid:** Miracle in Stone (256 pp. illus.)(4" x 7")	Seiss
017-0	**Jacob Boehme:** Life and Doctrines (352 pp.)	Hartmann
042-1	**Liberty Bell Papers:** The American Bi-Centennial (96 pp.)	Moore
229-7	**Meditations on the Signs of the Zodiac** (288 pp. illus.)	Jocelyn
206-8	**Mysticism at the Dawn of the Modern Age** (256 pp.)	Steiner
230-0	**Occult & Curative Powers of Precious Stones** (496 pp.)	Fernie
234-3	**Paracelsus:** Life and Prophecies (320 pp. illus.)	Hartmann
208-4	**Philosophy of Spiritual Activity** (304 pp.)	Steiner
231-9	**Pictorial Key to the Tarot** (352 pp. illus)	Waite
200-9	**PK: A Report on Psycho-Kinesis** (320 pp. illus.)	Brown
019-7	**Real History of the Rosicrucians** (456 pp. illus.)	Waite
221-1	**Reincarnation and Immortality** (224 pp.)(4" x 7")	Steiner
210-6	**Rudolf Steiner:** An Autobiography (560 pp. illus.)	Steiner
211-4	**Spiritual Research:** Methods and Results (288 pp.)	Steiner
225-4	**Steinerbooks Dictionary of the Paranormal** (370 pp.)	Riland
212-2	**Truth and Knowledge:** (112 pp.)	Steiner
244-0	**Unknown Philosopher:** Louis Claude de St. Martin (464 pp.)	Waite
213-0	**Vladimir Soloviev:** Russian Mystic (512 pp. illus.)	Allen

Spiritual Fiction Publications

Trade Paperbacks: 5⅜" x 8¼"

ISBN: 0-8334

0019-3	**Brother of the Third Degree** (384 pp.)	Garver
0020-7	**Hypatia** (416 pp.)	Kingsley
0024-X	**Legend** (304 pp.)	Maher
0018-5	**Romance of Two Worlds** (320 pp.)	Corelli
0015-0	**Seraphita** (216 pp.)	Balzac
0016-9	**Vril** (256 pp.)	Bulwer-Lytton
0021-5	**Death of the Gods** (464 pp.)	Merejkowski
0025-8	**Golem:** Mystical Tales from Prague Ghetto (248 pp.)	Bloch
0017-7	**Zanoni:** A Rosicrucian Tale (416 pp.)	Bulwer/Lytton
0022-3	**Dweller on Two Planets** (432 pp.)	Phylos the Thibetan

Spiritual Research Editions

Trade Paperbacks: 8" x 10"

ISBN: 0-8334

2020-8	**Earthly Death and Cosmic Life** (84 pp.)	Steiner
2021-6	**Evolution in the Aspect of Realities** (76 pp.)	Steiner
2022-4	**The Mission of Folk Souls** (164 pp.)	Steiner

Garber Communications, Inc., 5 Garber Hill Rd., Blauvelt, N.Y. 10913. U.S.A.
Send 50¢ for complete catalog.

Spiritual Science Library

Selected Classics of the Spiritual Sciences in Hardcover Buckram Library Editions.
Uniform 5½" x 8½" (unless otherwise noted).   ISBN Prefix: 0-89345

047-2	An Esoteric Cosomology (144 pp.)	Steiner and Schure
009-X	Christian Rosenkreutz Anthology (640 pp. profusely illus., oversize 8½" x 11¼")	Allen
021-9	Christianity & the Occult Mysteries of Antiquity (256 pp.)	Steiner
022-7	Cosmic Memory: Atlantis and Lemuria (272 pp.)	Steiner
039-1	Dweller on Two Planets (432 pp. illus.)	Phylos the Thibetan
055-3	Earthly and Cosmic Man (176 pp.)	Steiner
056-1	East in the Light of the West (376 pp.) (plus the drama: Children of Lucifer by E. Schure)	Steiner
024-3	Education As An Art (128 pp.)	Steiner
060-X	Evolution of the World and of Humanity (264 pp.)	Steiner
033-2	Fredrich Nietzsche: Fighter For Freedom (224 pp.)	Steiner
011-1	From Sphinx To Christ: An Occult History (288 pp.)	Schure
025-1	Great Initiates: Secret History of Religions (528 pp.)	Schure
016-2	Jacob Boehme: Life and Doctrines (352 pp.)	Hartmann
036-7	Life and Work of Rudolf Steiner (644 pp. illus. 6¼" x 9¼")	Wachsmuth
057-X	Man in the Light of Occultism, Theosophy, Philosophy (216 pp.)	Steiner
027-8	Meditations on the Signs of the Zodiac (288 pp. illus.)	Jocelyn
059-6	Mysteries of the East and of Christianity (96 pp.)	Steiner
026-X	Mysticism at the Dawn of the Modern Age (256 pp.)	Steiner
029-4	Our Inheritance in the Great Pyramid (672 pp. illus.)	Smyth
030-8	Philosophy of Spiritual Activity (304 pp.)	Steiner
041-3	Pistis Sophia: A Gnostic Gospel (408 pp.)	Mead
012-X	Portal of Initiation (288 pp. illus.)	Steiner
018-9	Real History of the Rosicrucians (456 pp. illus.)	Waite
031-6	Rudolf Steiner: An Autobiography (560 pp. illus.)	Steiner
020-0	Self-Consciousness: The Spiritual Human Being (328 pp.)	Steiner
058-8	Spiritual Ground of Education (144 pp.)	Steiner
010-3	Spiritual Research: Methods and Results (288 pp.)	Steiner
028-6	Steinerbooks Dictionary of the Paranormal (370 pp.)	Riland
008-1	Truth and Knowledge: Introduction to Spiritual Activity (112 pp.)	Steiner
048-0	Turning Points in Spiritual History (304 pp.)	Steiner
032-4	Vladimir Soloviev: Russian Mystic (544 pp. illus.)	Allen
014-6	Zanoni: A Rosicrucian Tale (416 pp.)	Bulwer-Lytton

Freedeeds Library   ISBN: 0-8334

Trade Editions: Hardcover (H.C.) or Paperback (P.B.) 5½" x 8½" (as noted)

050-2	American Mercury Magazine: Facsimile Edition of Vol. 1 Issues of Jan., Feb., Mar., April 1924 (600 pp. illus. 7" x 10" H.C.)	Mencken, etal
040-5	Citizens of the Cosmos (198 pp. illus., 6" x 9" H.C.)	Jocelyn
043-X	Liberty Bell Papers: The American Bi-Centennial (96 pp. H.C.)	Moore
013-8	PK: A Report on Psycho-Kinesis (320 pp. illus. H.C.)	Brown
004-9	Shards From the Heart: A Spiritual Odyssey (160 pp. H.C.)	Garber
1000-8	Buddha: A Pictorial History (272 pp. illus. 9" x 12", H.C. Deluxe Edition)	Auboyer
1001-6	Sacred Texts of the World: A Universal Anthology (496 pp. illus. 7¼" x 9¾", P.B.)	Smart & Hecht
1002-4	Return of the Goddess (288 pp. P.B.)	Whitmont
1003-2	Spiritual in Art (436 pp., 532 illus., 10" x 10")	Tuchman
1004-0	A Passionate Love of Mankind (104 pp.)	Kitt

Rudolf Steiner Publications

Russian Language Edition, Soft-Cover, Mimeographed 8½" x 11"   ISBN 0-89345

900-3	Gospel of St. John (Cassel) (294 pp.)	Steiner
901-1	Mysticism at the Dawn of the Modern Age (102 pp.)	Steiner